EQUINOX

A MODERN COTTON COLLECTION

By Knit Picks

Photography by John Cranford

Printed in the United States of America

First Printing, 2020

ISBN 978-1-62767-263-4

Versa Press, Inc.
800-447-7829

www.versapress.com

CONTENTS

BIRDIE TOP

by Katie Noseworthy

FINISHED MEASUREMENTS

32.25 (36, 39.75, 44, 47.75, 52, 56.25)"
finished bust circumference; meant to
be worn with 2-4" positive ease
Sample is 39.75" size; model is 33.5" bust

YARN

Lindy Chain™ (fingering weight, 70%
Linen, 30% Pima Cotton; 180 yards/50g):
Blue 27001, 5 (6, 6, 7, 8, 8, 9) balls

NEEDLES

US 4 (3.5mm) 24" circular needles,
and 32" circular needles for Magic
Loop technique or DPNs, or size to
obtain gauge

NOTIONS

Yarn Needle
Two Stitch Markers
Cable Needle
Scrap Yarn, Spare Needle,
or Stitch Holder
Blocking Pins and/or Wires

GAUGE

22 sts and 28 rnds = 4" in Stockinette
Stitch in the round, blocked

For pattern support, contact katie@knitsprite.com

Birdie Top

Notes:

Birdie is the perfect top for those warm summer days, whether you're relaxing in the yard or hard at work in the office!

This lightweight top features a simple eyelet lace pattern that converges to a point on the back, with some slight eyelet detailing along the front neckband. It's worked from the bottom up, with high-low shaping to add some flair to this otherwise classic top. Finally, knitters can choose to make a tank or tee version, with instructions for each included in the pattern.

Eyelet patterns are both written and charted. Charts are worked flat; only RS rows (odd numbers) are shown on charts—read all chart rows from right to left. All WS rows (even numbers) are worked: P across.

German Short Rows

RS Instructions: Knit to st specified in pattern. Turn work and Sl first st from LH needle to RH needle WYIF. Pull yarn to back of work over the top of RH needle, making it look as if there are 2 sts instead of 1. (This "double stitch" will be referred to as the *turn stitch* in instructions). Bring yarn to front between needles to begin purling.

WS Instructions: Purl to st specified in pattern. Turn work and bring yarn to front between the needles. Sl first st from LH needle to RH needle WYIF. Pull yarn to back of work over the top of RH needle, making it look as if there are 2 sts instead of 1 (the *turn stitch*). You are now ready to knit.

Eyelet Chart A (flat over 45 sts)
Row 1 (RS): K22, YO, SSK, K21.
Row 2 and all WS Rows: P across.
Row 3: K across.
Row 5: K19, YO, SSK, K4, YO, SSK, K18.
Row 7: K across.
Row 9: K16, (YO, SSK, K4) two times, YO, SSK, K15.
Row 11: K across.
Row 13: K13, (YO, SSK, K4) three times, YO, SSK, K12.
Row 15: K across.
Row 17: K10, (YO, SSK, K4) four times, YO, SSK, K9.
Row 19: K across.
Row 21: K7, (YO, SSK, K4) five times, YO, SSK, K6.
Row 23: K across.
Row 25: K4, (YO, SSK, K4) six times, YO, SSK, K3.
Row 27: K across.
Row 29: K1, (YO, SSK, K4) seven times, YO, SSK.
Row 31: K across.
Row 33: Rep Row 25.
Row 35: K across.
Row 37: Rep Row 29.

Eyelet Chart B (flat starting with 55 sts)
Row 1 (RS): K27, YO, K28. 56 sts.
Row 2 and all WS Rows: P across.
Row 3: K across.
Row 5: K24, YO, SSK, K4, YO, SSK, K24.
Row 7: K across.
Row 9: K21, (YO, SSK, K4) two times, YO, SSK, K21.
Row 11: K across.
Row 13: K18, (YO, SSK, K4) three times, YO, SSK, K18.
Row 15: K across.
Row 17: K15, (YO, SSK, K4) four times, YO, SSK, K15.
Row 19: K across.
Row 21: K12, (YO, SSK, K4) five times, YO, SSK, K12.
Row 23: K across.
Row 25: K9, (YO, SSK, K4) six times, YO, SSK, K9.
Row 27: K across.
Row 29: K6, (YO, SSK, K4) seven times, YO, SSK, K6.
Row 31: K across.
Row 33: K3, (YO, SSK, K4) eight times, YO, SSK, K3.
Row 35: K across.
Row 37: (YO, SSK, K4) nine times, YO, SSK.

Eyelet Chart C (flat starting with 65 sts)
Row 1 (RS): K32, YO, K33. 66 sts.
Row 2 and all WS Rows: P across.
Row 3: K across.
Row 5: K29, YO, SSK, K4, YO, SSK, K29.
Row 7: K across.
Row 9: K26, (YO, SSK, K4) two times, YO, SSK, K26.
Row 11: K across.
Row 13: K23, (YO, SSK, K4) three times, YO, SSK, K23.
Row 15: K across.
Row 17: K20, (YO, SSK, K4) four times, YO, SSK, K20.
Row 19: K across.
Row 21: K17, (YO, SSK, K4) five times, YO, SSK, K17.
Row 23: K across.
Row 25: K14, (YO, SSK, K4) six times, YO, SSK, K14.
Row 27: K across.
Row 29: K11, (YO, SSK, K4) seven times, YO, SSK, K11.
Row 31: K across.
Row 33: K8, (YO, SSK, K4) eight times, YO, SSK, K8.
Row 35: K across.
Row 37: K5, (YO, SSK, K4) nine times, YO, SSK, K5.
Row 39: K across.
Row 41: K2, (YO, SSK, K4) ten times, YO, SSK, K2.
Row 43: K across.
Row 45: Rep Row 37.
Row 47: K across.
Row 49: Rep Row 41.

DIRECTIONS

Body

CO 194 (214, 234, 258, 278, 302, 326) sts using the Long Tail Cast On method. Join in the rnd, being careful not to twist sts.

Setup Rnd: PM for BOR, P97 (107, 117, 129, 139, 151, 163), PM, P97 (107, 117, 129, 139, 151, 163). The first 97 (107, 117, 129, 139, 151, 163) sts are the front, the second, the back. Ms indicate left and right sides, respectively.

Work Garter Stitch for ten rnds.
Knit three rnds.

German Short Row Bottom Shaping

Short Row 1 (RS): K31 (36, 39, 45, 47, 53, 57), turn.
Short Row 2 (WS): P to BOR, SM, P across back sts, SM, P31 (36, 39, 45, 47, 53, 57), turn. 35 (35, 39, 39, 45, 45, 49) sts remain unworked on front.
Short Row 3: K to 3 sts before turn st, turn.
Short Row 4: P to 3 sts before turn st, turn.
Work Short Rows 3–4 16 (18, 20, 23, 24, 27, 29) times total. 31 (35, 35, 35, 41, 41, 45) sts remain between turn sts at center back.

Body Middle

Next Row (RS): K to BOR.
Resume working in the rnd.
Knit one rnd. When working turn sts, work them tog as 1 st. WE in St st until piece measures 9 (9, 10, 10, 11, 11,12)″ from side of CO edge (or 6″ shorter than desired length).

Upper Body Shaping

Rnd 1: (K1, SSK, K to 3 sts before M, K2tog, K1, SM) two times. 4 sts dec.
Rnds 2–7: K all.
Rep Rnds 1–7 three more times. 178 (198, 218, 242, 262, 286, 310) sts.
WE in St st until piece measures 15 (15, 16, 16, 17, 17, 18)″ from side of CO edge, or to desired length.

Divide Front and Back

Setup Rnd: K to 3 (3, 4, 5, 6, 7, 8) sts before BOR, BO 3 (3, 4, 5, 6, 7, 8) sts, remove M. 175 (195, 214, 237, 256, 279, 302) sts.
Next Rnd: BO 3 (3, 4, 5, 6, 7, 8) sts, K to 3 (3, 4, 5, 6, 7, 8) sts before M, BO 3 (3, 4, 5, 6, 7, 8) sts, remove M, BO 3 (3, 4, 5, 6, 7, 8) sts, K to end. 166 (186, 202, 222, 238, 258, 278) sts.

K83 (93, 101, 111, 119, 129, 139), then place these Front sts onto scrap yarn or spare needle (or knit them directly onto spare needle); cont with 83 (93, 101, 111, 119, 129, 139) Back sts.

Back

Setup Row (RS): K19 (19, 23, 28, 27, 32, 37), PM, K45 (55, 55, 55, 65, 65, 65), PM, K19 (19, 23, 28, 27, 32, 37). These Ms will indicate strap placement later.

Armhole Shaping

Row 1 (RS): K1, SSK, K to last 3 sts, K2tog, K1. 2 sts dec.
Row 2 (WS): P across.
Work Rows 1–2 a total of 1 (2, 3, 5, 1, 3, 1) time(s). 81 (89, 95, 101, 117, 123, 137) sts.

Cont shaping armholes while simultaneously working Eyelet Chart A (B, B, B, C, C, C).
Work the following Rows 1–2 a total of 1 (0, 1, 3, 4, 4, 10) time(s).
Row 1 (RS): K1, SSK, K to M, SM, work Chart A (B, B, B, C, C, C), SM, K to last 3 sts, K2tog, K1. 2 sts dec.
Row 2 (WS): P across.
After reps, 79 (90, 94, 96, 110, 116, 118) sts; 17 (17, 19, 20, 22, 25, 26) sts for each strap, 45 (56, 56, 56, 66, 66, 66) sts between Ms for chart.

Next RS Row: K to M, SM, work Eyelet Chart A (B, B, B, C, C, C), SM, K to end.
Next WS Row: P across.
Work these two rows until Eyelet Chart is complete.

Neck Shaping

Setup Row (RS): K to M, remove M, BO 45 (56, 56, 56, 66, 66, 66) sts, remove M, K to end. 17 (17, 19, 20, 22, 25, 26) sts for each strap.
At this point, each strap will be worked separately. Place live sts for right strap on scrap yarn or st holder. Begin working left strap.

Back Left Strap Shaping

Row 1 (WS): P to last 3 sts, P2tog, P1. 1 st dec.
Row 2 (RS): K across.
Work Rows 1–2 a total of 2 (2, 2, 3, 3, 4, 4) times. 15 (15, 17, 17, 19, 21, 22) sts.
Work St st for 4 (4, 4, 2, 2, 0, 0) rows. Break yarn, leaving a 6″ tail. Place live sts on scrap yarn or st holder.

Back Right Strap Shaping

Place live sts back on needle.
Row 1 (RS): K to last 3 sts, K2tog, K1. 1 st dec.
Row 2 (WS): P across.
Work Rows 1–2 a total of 2 (2, 2, 3, 3, 4, 4) times. 15 (15, 17, 17, 19, 21, 22) sts.
Work St st for 4 (4, 4, 2, 2, 0, 0) rows. Break yarn, leaving a 6″ tail. Place live sts on scrap yarn or st holder.

Front

Setup Row (RS): K23 (26, 28, 33, 35, 38, 43), PM, K37 (41, 45, 45, 49, 53, 53), PM, K23 (26, 28, 33, 35, 38, 43). These Ms will indicate strap placement later.

Row 1 (RS): K1, SSK, K to last 3 sts, K2tog, K1. 2 sts dec.
Row 2 (WS): Purl across.
Work Rows 1–2 a total of 2 (2, 4, 8, 5, 7, 11) times. 79 (89, 93, 95, 109, 115, 117) sts.
Work St st for 18 (22, 22, 18, 26, 26, 22) rows, ending after a WS row.

Eyelet Row (RS): K to M, SM, K3 (2, 1, 1, 3, 2, 2), (YO, SSK, K4) 5 (6, 7, 7, 7, 8, 8) times, YO, SSK, K2 (1, 0, 0, 2, 1, 1), SM, K to end.
Next Row (WS): P across.

Neck Shaping

Setup Row (RS): K to M, remove M, BO 37 (41, 45, 45, 49, 53, 53) sts, remove M, K to end. 21 (24, 24, 25, 30, 31, 32) sts for each strap.

At this point, each strap will be worked separately. Place live sts for left strap on scrap yarn or st holder. Begin working right strap.

Front Right Strap Shaping
Row 1 (WS): P to last 3 sts, P2tog, P1. 1 st dec.
Row 2 (RS): K across.
Row 3: P to last 5 sts, P2tog, YO, P2tog, P1. 1 st dec.
Row 4: Rep Row 2.
Row 5: Rep Row 1. 1 st dec.
Row 6: Rep Row 2.
Work Rows 1–6 a total of 2 (3, 2, 2, 3, 3, 3) times. 15 (15, 18, 19, 21, 22, 23) sts.
Rep Rows 1–2 0 (0, 1, 2, 2, 1, 1) more time(s). 15 (15, 17, 17, 19, 21, 22) sts.
Work St st for 10 (3, 5, 6, 0, 1, 1) row(s). Break yarn, leaving a 6″ tail. Place live sts on scrap yarn or st holder.

Front Left Strap Shaping
Row 1 (RS): K to last 3 sts, SSK, K1. 1 st dec.
Row 2 (WS): P across.
Row 3: K to last 5 sts, SSK, YO, SSK, K1. 1 st dec.
Row 4: Rep Row 2.
Row 5: Rep Row 1. 1 st dec.
Row 6: Rep Row 2.
Work Rows 1–6 a total of 2 (3, 2, 2, 3, 3, 3) times. 15 (15, 18, 19, 21, 22, 23) sts.
Rep Rows 1–2 0 (0, 1, 2, 2, 1, 1) more time(s). 15 (15, 17, 17, 19, 21, 22) sts.
Work St st for 10 (3, 5, 6, 0, 1, 1) row(s). Break yarn, leaving a 6″ tail.

Graft front and back straps together using Kitchener stitch.

Sleeves
Right Sleeve
Using Magic Loop technique or DPNs, starting at middle of underarm sts, PU and K 38 (40, 44, 47, 51, 54, 58) sts along edge of back at a rate of approx 3 sts for every 4 rows. PU and K 1 st at the very top to close gap. PU and K 38 (40, 44, 47, 51, 54, 58) sts along edge of front. PM for BOR and join to work in the rnd. 77 (81, 89, 95, 103, 109, 117) sts.
Work Garter Stitch for four rnds.

Tank Version Only
BO loosely.

T-Shirt Version Only
The Garter Stitch cap sleeves are shaped using short rows. For this section, simply turn work instead of using German Short Rows method.
Short Row 1 (RS): K to 3 sts before BOR, turn.
Short Row 2 (WS): K to 3 sts before BOR, turn.
Short Row 3: K to 3 sts before gap, turn.
Short Row 4: K to 3 sts before gap, turn.
Rep Short Rows 3–4 seven more times.

Cont working in the rnd in Garter Stitch. *Note:* There is no need to do anything to close up short row gaps as the Garter st will fill them.

Work Garter Stitch until sleeve cap measures 2.5 (2.5, 3, 3, 3, 3.5, 3.5)″ from top seam.
BO loosely.

Left Sleeve
Rep instructions for right sleeve, starting at underarm and working up front then down back of garment.

Neck
Using Magic Loop technique or DPNs, starting at right shoulder seam on back, PU and K 6 (6, 6, 6, 6, 6, 6) sts along back right strap, PU and K 45 (56, 56, 56, 66, 66, 66) sts along back center BO sts, PU and K 6 (6, 6, 6, 6, 6, 6) sts along back left strap, PU and K 1 st in left shoulder seam to close gap, PU and K 22 (22, 22, 22, 22, 22, 22) sts along front left strap, PU and K 37 (41, 45, 45, 49, 53, 53) sts along front center BO sts, PU and K 22 (22, 22, 22, 22, 22, 22) sts along front right strap, PU and K 1 st in right shoulder seam to close gap. PM for BOR and join to knit in the rnd. 140 (155, 159, 159, 173, 177, 177) sts.

Work Garter Stitch for five rnds.
BO loosely K-wise and break yarn, leaving a 6″ tail.

Finishing
Weave in ends, wash, and block gently. For best results, use blocking wires to prevent the fabric from puckering at the edges.

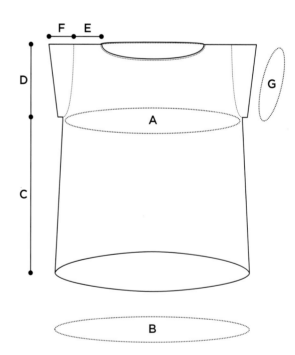

A   32.25 (36, 39.75, 44, 47.75, 52, 56.25)″
B   35.25 (39, 42.5, 47, 50.5, 55, 59.25)″
C   15 (15, 16, 16, 17, 17, 18)″
D   6.75 (7, 7.25, 7.75, 8.5, 9, 9.5)″
E   2.75 (2.75, 3, 3, 3.5, 3.75, 4)″
F   2.5 (2.5, 3, 3, 3, 3.5, 3.5)″
G   14 (14.75, 16.25, 17.25, 18.75, 19.75, 21.25)″

Eyelet Chart A

Eyelet Chart B

LEGEND

	Knit Stitch
O	YO — Yarn over
/	SSK — Slip, slip, knit slipped stitches together

Eyelet Chart C

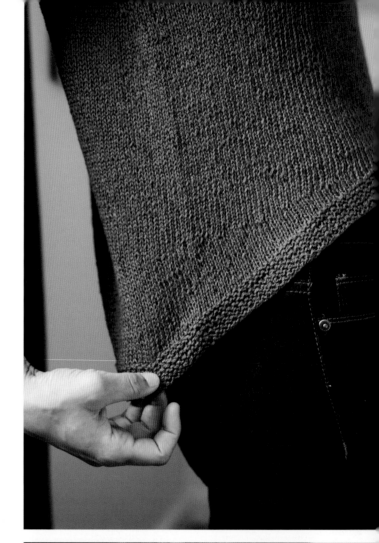

CASCADES TEE

by Emily Kintigh

FINISHED MEASUREMENTS

32.5 (36.5, 40.5, 44.5, 48.5, 52.5, 56.5, 60.5)" finished bust circumference; meant to be worn with no ease
Sample is 36.5" size; model is 33.5" bust

YARN

CotLin™ (DK weight, 70% Tanguis Cotton, 30% Linen; 123 yards/50g): Conch 25776, 5 (6, 7, 8, 9, 9, 11, 12) skeins

NEEDLES

US 7 (4.5 mm) straight or circular needles (24" or longer), and DPNs, or size to obtain gauge

NOTIONS

Yarn Needle
Stitch Markers
Locking Stitch Markers
Scrap Yarn

GAUGE

20 sts and 28 rows = 4" in Stockinette Stitch, blocked

For pattern support, contact auntieemsstudio@gmail.com

Cascades Tee

Notes:

This gorgeous tee features a lovely lace pattern that resembles mountains, starting at the neckline and continuing over the shoulders and along the top of the back. It has simple eyelet borders at the bottom hems and around the sleeves. This beautiful and versatile tee can easily be worn with skirts or jeans.

The tee is worked flat from the bottom front hem to the back hem with stitches placed on scrap yarn to be picked up for the neckline. The sides are then seamed and stitches are picked up to work the eyelet borders on the sleeves and the purl neckline in the round.

Chart is worked flat; read RS rows (odd numbers) from right to left, and WS rows (even numbers) from left to right.

DIRECTIONS

Body Front
Loosely CO 83 (93, 103, 113, 123, 133, 143, 153) sts.
Rows 1-3: K across.
Row 4 (WS): K3, (P2tog, YO) to last 4 sts, P1, K3.
Rows 5-7: K across.
Row 8: K3, P to last 3 sts, K3.
Row 9: K across.
Rows 10-11: Rep Rows 8-9.
Row 12: P across.
Cont in St st until piece measures 18.25 (18.25, 18.75, 19.5, 21, 21, 22.5, 23.25)" from CO edge, ending with a WS row.

Neckline
Begin working from Cascades Chart as follows. Sts are worked on either end of each row in St st, while chart is repeated in middle. If desired, use Ms between reps.

Row 1 (RS): K1, PM, work Row 1 of Cascades Chart to last 2 sts, PM, K2.
Row 2 (WS): P2, SM, work Row 2 of Cascades Chart to last st, SM, P1.
Row 3: K1, SM, work next row of Cascades Chart to last 2 sts, SM, K2.
Row 4: P2, SM, work next row of Cascades Chart to last st, SM, P1.
Cont as established; after working Cascades Chart Rows 3-4, begin working reps of Cascades Chart Rows 5-8, until piece measures 22.25 (22.25, 22.75, 24, 26, 26, 28, 28.75)" from CO edge, ending with a RS row.

Neck Opening
Next Row (WS): P16 (21, 26, 30, 35, 40, 44, 49); using scrap yarn, P51 (51, 51, 53, 53, 53, 55, 55), then Sl these sts back to LH needle; cont with working yarn, P to end. This row replaces next WS row of chart.

Back
Cont with next RS row as established for Neckline. Cont working Rows 5-8 of Cascades Chart until piece measures 7.5 (7.5, 7.5, 8, 8.5, 8.5, 9, 9)" from Neck Opening, ending with a chart Row 8.
Work Rows 9-12 of Cascades Chart. Remove Ms.

Work St st until piece measures 20.75 (20.75, 21.25, 22.5, 24.5, 24.5, 26.5, 27.25)" from Neck Opening, ending with a RS row.

Hem
Row 1 (WS): K3, P to last 3 sts, K3.
Row 2 (RS): K across.
Rows 3-4: Rep Rows 1-2.
Rows 5-6: K across.
Row 7: K3, (P2tog, YO) to last 4 sts, P1, K3.
Rows 8-9: K across.
BO all sts.

Fold in half so CO and BO edges meet. Seam both sides using Mattress Stitch, starting 1.5" from CO and BO edges and working until 16.25 (16.25, 16.25, 17, 18.25, 18.25, 18.5, 18.5)" from CO and BO edges.

Sleeve (make two the same)
PU and K 60 (60, 66, 70, 78, 78, 96, 102) sts around armhole. PM for BOR and join to work in the rnd.
Rnd 1: P all.
Rnd 2: K all.
Rnd 3: (YO, K2tog) to end.
Rnd 4: K all.
Rnd 5: P all.
BO all sts.

Neck Edging
PU the 51 (51, 51, 53, 53, 53, 55, 55) sts on either side of scrap yarn, removing scrap yarn. 102 (102, 102, 106, 106, 110, 110) sts total. PM for BOR and join to work in the rnd.
Rnd 1: P all.
BO all sts.

Finishing
Weave in ends, wash, and block to diagram.

Cascades Chart

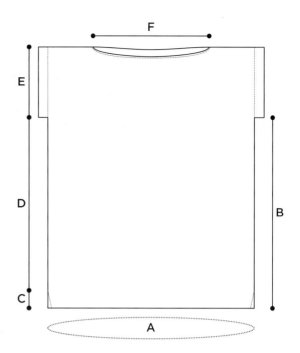

LEGEND

K
RS: Knit stitch
WS: Purl stitch

YO
Yarn over

K2tog
Knit 2 stitches together as one stitch

SSK
Slip, slip, knit slipped stitches together

SK2P
Slip 1 knit-wise, K2tog, pass slip stitch over K2tog

Pattern Repeat

A   32.5 (36.5, 40.5, 44.5, 48.5, 52.5, 56.5, 60.5)"
B   16.25 (16.25, 16.25, 17, 18.25, 18.25, 18.5, 18.5)"
C   1.5"
D   14.75 (14.75, 14.75, 15.5, 16.75, 16.75, 17, 17)"
E   6 (6, 6.5, 7, 7.75, 7.75, 9.5, 10.25)"
F   10.25 (10.25, 10.25, 10.5, 10.5, 10.5, 11, 11)"

DAISY SWEATER

by Violet LeBeaux

FINISHED MEASUREMENTS

39.25 (40.75, 42.5, 44, 45.5, 47.25)"
finished hip circumference; meant to
be worn with 2–4" positive ease
*Sample is 40.75" size; model is 33.5"
bust, 37.25" hip*

YARN

Comfy™ (worsted weight, 75% Pima
Cotton, 25% Acrylic; 109 yards/50g):
Lilac Mist 28014, 13 (13, 14, 14, 15, 15)
skeins

NEEDLES

US 6 (4mm) straight or circular needles
(32" or longer), or size to obtain gauge

NOTIONS

Yarn Needle
Stitch Markers
Scrap Yarn or Stitch Holder
Sewing Needle and Thread
Blocking Pins and/or Wires

GAUGE

20 sts and 26 rows = 4" in Lace Stitch
and Stockinette Stitch, blocked

For pattern support, contact violetlebeaux@gmail.com

Daisy Sweater

Notes:

Daisy is a fashionable oversized sweater that is great for spring weather or even as a beach cover up! It features sections of simple mesh trellis lace between Stockinette Stitch, a curved hem, and dolman sleeves. The wide neckband allows for wearing off the shoulder and the relaxed fit is perfect with jeans.

Construction is bottom up, with front and back worked flat separately then seamed together. Ribbing for the sleeves is added at the end. The lace is a simple 4-row repeat that is easy to remember for experienced knitters and fun for beginners.

Short rows are worked at the bottom of the sweater; use any preferred short row technique, such as W&T or German Short Rows, when short rows are worked.

Lace Stitch (flat over an even number of sts)
Row 1 (RS): (K2tog, YO) to end.
Row 2 (WS): P across.
Row 3: (YO, SSK) to end.
Row 4: P across.
Rep Rows 1–4 for pattern.

DIRECTIONS

Front Body
Hem Flap
This piece is worked flat and creates the curved ribbed hem at the bottom of the sweater.
Loosely CO 98 (102, 106, 110, 114, 118) sts.
Work 2x2 Rib for eight rows.

Short Rows
Short Row 1 (RS): Sl1, K to last 2 sts, turn.
Short Row 2 (WS): Sl1, P to last 2 sts, turn.
Work Short Rows 1–2 three more times, working 2 fewer sts each row.

Row 1 (RS): K across.
Row 2 (WS): P across.
Rep Rows 1–2 once more.
Knit two rows.

Lace Increase Section
Row 1 (RS): K2, YO, work Lace Stitch, beginning with Rnd 1, to last 2 sts, K1, YO, K1. 2 sts inc.
Row 2 (WS): P2, YO, P1, work Lace Stitch to last 3 sts, P2, YO, P1. 2 sts inc.
Row 3: K2, work Lace Stitch to last 2 sts, K2.
Row 4: P2, work Lace Stitch to last 2 sts, P2.
Rep Rows 1–4 four more times. 118 (122, 126, 130, 134, 138) sts.

Plain Increase Section
Row 1 (RS): K2, M1, K to last 2 sts, M1, K2. 2 sts inc.
Row 2 (WS): K across.
Row 3: Rep Row 1. 2 sts inc.
Row 4: P across.
Rep Rows 3–4 eight more times.
Rep Rows 1–2 once. 140 (144, 148, 152, 156, 160) sts.

Repeats
Rep Lace Increase Section and Plain Increase Section two more times. 224 (228, 232, 236, 240, 244) sts.

Lace Arms Section
This section continues the lace without increasing the width, so the edges of the sleeves are flat.
Row 1 (RS): K2, work Lace Stitch, beginning with Rnd 1, to last 2 sts, K2.
Row 2 (WS): P2, work Lace Stitch to last 2 sts, P2.
Rep Rows 1–2 nine more times.
Cont to either Front or Back Neckband section.

Front Neckband
Rows 1–2: K across.
Work St st for 0 (2, 4, 6, 8, 10) rows.
Next Row (RS): K77 (79, 79, 81, 81, 83), (P2, K2) for 70 (70, 74, 74, 78, 78) sts, K to end.
Next Row (WS): P77 (79, 79, 81, 81, 83), (K2, P2) for 70 (70, 74, 74, 78, 78) sts, P to end.
Work as established for six more rows.
BO all sts.

Back
Work as for Front Body through the Lace Arms Section, then cont to Back Neckband section.

Back Neckband
This section creates the back neckband including the flap of ribbing that joins to the front neckband.
Rows 1–2: K across.
Work St st for 8 (10, 12, 14, 16, 18) rows.
BO first and last 77 (79, 79, 81, 81, 83) sts, leaving middle 70 (70, 74, 74, 78, 78) sts on needles.
Work 2x2 Rib for 8 rows.
BO all sts.

Cuff (make two the same)
Ribbed cuffs are worked flat and seamed to ends of sleeves.
Loosely CO 36 (36, 40, 40, 40, 44) sts.
Work 2x2 Rib for eight rows.
BO all sts.

Finishing
Lay front and back pieces of sweater flat tog and sew along shoulder/arm seams. Fit and sew Cuff pieces to armholes. Sew from edge of cuff to hem. Tuck Back Neckband edge under Front Neckband edge so ribbing overlaps, sew in place. Weave in ends, wash, and block to diagram.

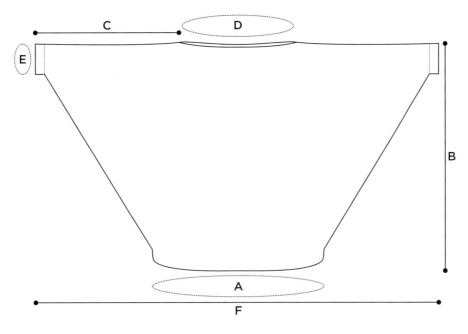

A 39.25 (40.75, 42.5, 44, 45.5, 47.25)"
B 26 (26.25, 26.5, 27, 27.25, 27.5)"
C 16.75 (17, 17, 17.5, 17.5, 17.57)"
D 28 (28, 29.5, 29.5, 31.25, 31.25)"
E 7 (7, 8, 8, 8, 9)"
F 47.25 (48, 49, 49.75, 50.5, 51.25)"

DECLARE PULLOVER

by Renate Kamm

FINISHED MEASUREMENTS

38 (42, 45.75, 49.5, 53.25, 57.25, 61)"
finished bust circumference; meant to
be worn with 2–4" positive ease
Sample is 38" size; model is 33.5" bust

YARN

Shine™ (sport weight, 60% Pima Cotton,
40% Modal® natural beech wood fiber;
110 yards/50g): Dandelion 25340, 8 (9,
10, 11, 12, 13, 14) skeins

NEEDLES

US 5 (3.75mm) 32" circular needles,
and DPNs or two 24" circular needles
for two circulars technique or 32" or
longer circular needles for Magic Loop
technique, or size to obtain gauge

NOTIONS

Yarn Needle
Stitch Markers
Removable Stitch Marker
Scrap Yarn or Stitch Holder

GAUGE

21 sts and 28 rnds = 4" in Stockinette
Stitch in the round, blocked

For pattern support, contact oberpfalzerin@hotmail.com

Declare Pullover

Notes:

Spring would not be the same without dandelions. Inspired by a love for these flowers, this pullover includes rows of dandelion stitches. Boxy and slightly cropped, Declare represents freedom of movement and practicality.

Split hems lead to a body knit in the round, decorated by rows of dandelion stitches. Front and back are completed separately. Shoulders are seamed before stitches are picked up for the three-quarter-length sleeves. Sleeves are also knit in the round, decorated with a row of opposite direction dandelion flower stitches.

Body Flowers (in the round over 8 sts)
Rnd 1: K3, knit into second st on LH needle three rows down, pull up a loop of working yarn, and place it on RH needle, K2, knit into same space as before and pull up another loop onto RH needle, K2, knit into same space as before and pull up a third loop onto RH needle, K1. 3 sts inc.
Rnd 2: K2, (K2tog, K1) three times. 3 sts dec.

Sleeve Flowers (in the round over 8 sts)
Rnd 1: K6, knit into second st on RH needle four rows down, pull up a loop of working yarn onto RH needle, knit into next st on LH needle three rows down, pull up a loop onto RH needle, knit into third st on LH needle three rows down, pull up a loop onto RH needle, K2. 3 sts inc.
Rnd 2: K6, CDD the 3 loops, K2tog. 3 sts dec.

Alternate Cable Cast On
Make a slip knot and place on LH needle. Place RH needle into slip knot K-wise and knit a st without dropping slip knot off LH needle, drawing through extra slack. Place new st on LH needle, and gently tighten. *Insert working needle between last 2 sts on LH needle from back to front and purl without dropping st off LH needle; place new st onto LH needle and gently tighten. Insert needle between last 2 sts on LH needle from front to back and knit without dropping st off LH needle; place new st on LH needle and gently tighten. Rep from * until required number of sts is reached.

DIRECTIONS

Hem
CO 101 (111, 121, 131, 141, 151, 161) sts using the Alternate Cable Cast On method.
Row 1 (RS): K1, (K1, P1) to end.
Row 2 (WS): K1, (P1, K1) to end.
Row 3: K1, (K1, P1) to last 2 sts, K1, Sl1.
Row 4: K1, (P1, K1) to last 2 sts, P1, Sl1.
Rep Rows 3–4 five more times, for a total of 14 rows.
Do not break yarn.

Make a second Hem.
Place both hem sections onto circular needles with RSs facing same direction, so that working yarn of first hem section is at first st. 202 (222, 242, 262, 282, 302, 322) sts. Break yarn of second hem section, leaving a 4″ tail.

Body
Join to work in the rnd by knitting the edge sts of both hem sections tog as follows.
Closing Rnd: Sl1, K to last st of first hem, K2tog (last st of first hem and first st of second hem) K to last st of second hem, K2tog (last st of second hem and first st of first hem). 200 (220, 240, 260, 280, 300, 320) sts. PM for BOR.

Rnds 1–4: K all.
Rnd 5: K2 (3, 4, 1, 2, 3, 4), work Body Flowers Rnd 1 12 (13, 14, 16, 17, 18, 19) times, K4 (6, 8, 2, 4, 6, 8), work Body Flowers Rnd 1 12 (13, 14, 16, 17, 18, 19) times, K2 (3, 4, 1, 2, 3, 4).
Rnd 6: K2 (3, 4, 1, 2, 3, 4), work Body Flowers Rnd 2 12 (13, 14, 16, 17, 18, 19) times, K4 (6, 8, 2, 4, 6, 8), work Body Flowers Rnd 2 12 (13, 14, 16, 17, 18, 19) times, K2 (3, 4, 1, 2, 3, 4).
Rnds 7–10: K all.
Rnd 11: K6 (7, 8, 5, 6, 7, 8) work Body Flowers Rnd 1 11 (12, 13, 15, 16, 17, 18) times, K12 (14, 16, 10, 12, 14, 16), work Body Flowers Rnd 1 11 (12, 13, 15, 16, 17, 18) times, K6 (7, 8, 5, 6, 7, 8).
Rnd 12: K6 (7, 8, 5, 6, 7, 8) work Body Flowers Rnd 2 11 (12, 13, 15, 16, 17, 18) times, K12 (14, 16, 10, 12, 14, 16), work Body Flowers Rnd 2 11 (12, 13, 15, 16, 17, 18) times, K6 (7, 8, 5, 6, 7, 8).
Rep Rnds 1–6 once.

Cont working in St st until 91 (91, 91, 98, 98, 98, 98) rnds have been worked after hem ribbing; piece measures approx 15 (15, 15, 16, 16, 16, 16)″ from CO edge.

Separate Front and Back
Mark space between last and first st for armhole with removable M or scrap yarn, K100 (110, 120, 130, 140, 150, 160), place just-worked sts on st holder or scrap yarn, mark space before next st for other armhole with removable M or scrap yarn, K to end.

Back
Work St st in rows, back and forth across 100 (110, 120, 130, 140, 150, 160) sts between Ms.
RS Rows: Sl1, K to end.
WS Rows: Sl1, P to end.
WE until armholes measure 5 (5.25, 5.75, 6, 6.75, 7.25, 8)″ from underarm, ending with a WS row. Approx 36 (38, 40, 42, 48, 50, 56) rows have been worked.

Shape Neck and Shoulders
Next Row (RS): BO 3 (3, 3, 5, 5, 5, 6) sts, K35 (37, 41, 44, 48, 52, 56), place just-worked sts on st holder or scrap yarn for Right Shoulder, BO 24 (30, 32, 32, 35, 36, 36) sts, K38 (40, 44, 49, 52, 57, 62) for Left Shoulder. Neck and shoulder shaping are now worked at the same time.

Left Shoulder

At beginning of WS rows, BO 3 (3, 3, 5, 5, 5, 6) sts 4 (4, 1, 7, 5, 1, 3) times, then BO 5 (5, 4, 0, 6, 6, 7) sts 3 (3, 2, 0, 2, 6, 4) times, then BO 0 (0, 5, 0, 0, 0, 0) sts 0 (0, 4, 0, 0, 0, 0) times. AT THE SAME TIME, at beginning of RS rows, BO 4 sts once, then BO 3 sts 0 (1, 1, 2, 2, 3, 3) times, then BO 2 sts 2 (2, 2, 1, 2, 1, 1) times, and BO 1 st 3 (2, 2, 2, 2, 1, 1) times. 0 sts.

Right Shoulder

Return 35 (37, 41, 44, 48, 52, 56) held Right Shoulder sts to needle and, with WS facing, rejoin yarn.

At beginning of WS rows, BO 4 sts once, then BO 3 sts 0 (1, 1, 2, 2, 3, 3) times, then BO 2 sts 2 (2, 2, 1, 2, 1, 1) times, then BO 1 st 3 (2, 2, 2, 2, 1, 1) times.

AT THE SAME TIME, at beginning of RS rows, BO 3 (3, 3, 5, 5, 5, 6) sts 3 (3, 0, 6, 4, 0, 2) times, then BO 5 (5, 4, 0, 6, 6, 7) sts 3 (3, 2, 0, 2, 6, 4) times, then BO 0 (0, 5, 0, 0, 0, 0) sts 0 (0, 4, 0, 0, 0, 0) times. 0 sts.

Front

Work St st in rows, back and forth. Move all 100 (110, 120, 130, 140, 150, 160) sts onto a long circular needle and attach yarn at first st with RS facing.

Shape Neck and Shoulders

Next Row (RS): K48 (53, 58, 63, 68, 73, 78), SSK, place just-worked sts on st holder or scrap yarn for Left Front, K2tog, K48 (53, 58, 63, 68, 73, 78). 49 (54, 59, 64, 69, 74, 79) sts.

Right Front

Next Row (WS): Sl1, P to last 2 sts, P2tog. 48 (53, 58, 63, 68, 73, 78) sts.

Dec Row (RS): Sl1, K1, K2tog, K to end. 1 st dec.

Next Row and all WS Rows: Sl1, P to end.

WE in St st and rep Dec Row every RS row 20 (25, 26, 27, 30, 31, 31) more times.

AT THE SAME TIME, begin BO for shoulder when armhole measures 5 (5.25, 5.75, 6, 6.75, 7.25, 8)". At beginning of WS rows, BO 3 (3, 3, 5, 5, 5, 6) sts 4 (4, 1, 7, 5, 1, 3) times, then BO 5 (5, 4, 0, 6, 6, 7) sts 3 (3, 2, 0, 2, 6, 4) times, then BO 0 (0, 5, 0, 0, 0, 0) sts 0 (0, 4, 0, 0, 0, 0) times. 0 sts.

Left Front

Return 49 (54, 59, 64, 69, 74, 79) held Left Front sts to needle and, with WS facing, attach yarn.

Next Row (WS): P2tog, P to last st, Sl1. 48 (53, 58, 63, 68, 73, 78) sts.

Dec Row (RS): K to last 4 sts, SSK, K1, Sl1. 1 st dec.

Next Row and all WS Rows: P to last st, Sl1.

WE in St st and rep Dec Row every RS row 20 (25, 26, 27, 30, 31, 31) more times.

AT THE SAME TIME, begin BO for shoulder when armhole measures 5 (5.25, 5.75, 6, 6.75, 7.25, 8)". At beginning of RS rows, BO 3 (3, 3, 5, 5, 5, 6) sts 4 (4, 1, 7, 5, 1, 3) times, then BO 5 (5, 4, 0, 6, 6, 7) sts 3 (3, 2, 0, 2, 6, 4) times, then BO 0 (0, 5, 0, 0, 0, 0) sts 0 (0, 4, 0, 0, 0, 0) times. 0 sts.

Sleeves (make two the same)

Sew shoulder seams.

With DPNs and RS facing, beginning at center of underarm, PU and K 54 (57, 62, 66, 72, 76, 84) sts, approx 3 sts for every 4 rows, evenly around armhole edge. PM and join in the rnd. Knit four rnds.

Dec Rnd: K1, K2tog, K to last 3 sts, SSK, K1. 2 sts dec.

Rep Dec Rnd every 24 (24, 24, 16, 24, 24, 12) rnds 2 (2, 2, 3, 2, 2, 4) more times. 48 (51, 56, 58, 66, 70, 74) sts.

Knit eight rnds.

Sleeve Flowers

Rnd 1: K0 (2, 0, 1, 1, 3, 1), work Sleeve Flowers Rnd 1 6 (6, 7, 7, 8, 8, 9) times, K0 (1, 0, 1, 1, 3, 1).

Rnd 2: K0 (2, 0, 1, 1, 3, 1), work Sleeve Flowers Rnd 2 6 (6, 7, 7, 8, 8, 9) times, K0 (1, 0, 1, 1, 3, 1).

Knit two rnds.

Cuff

Rnds 1–14: (K1, P1) to end, ending with P1 (K1, P1, P1, P1, P1, P1).

BO all sts.

Neckband

Starting at front center with RS facing, PU and K 44 (46, 48, 50, 55, 59, 63) sts up right V-neck edge, PU and K 48 (56, 58, 60, 66, 68, 68) sts across back neck edge, PU and K 44 (46, 48, 50, 55, 59, 63) sts down left V-neck edge, turn (do not join). Neck band is worked in rows, back and forth. 136 (148, 154, 160, 176, 186, 194) sts.

Setup Row (WS): Sl1, (P1, K1) 21 (22, 23, 24, 27, 29, 31) times, P1 (0, 0, 0, 0, 0, 0), P2tog 0 (1, 1, 1, 1, 1, 1) time, (K1, P1, K1, P2tog) three times, (K1, P1) 4 (8, 9, 10, 13, 14, 14) times, (K1, P1, K1, P2tog) 3 (4, 4, 4, 4, 4, 4) times, (K1, P1) to last 2 sts, K1, Sl1. 130 (140, 146, 152, 168, 178, 186) sts.

Row 1 (RS): K1, (P1, K1) to last st, K1.

Row 2 (WS): Sl1, (P1, K1) to last st, Sl1.

Rep Rows 1–2 three more times, for total of eight rows, 1.25" of ribbing.

BO all sts using Jeny's Surprisingly Stretchy Bind Off for 1x1 Rib.

Finishing

Sew left edge of Neckband to right V-neck edge, and then sew right edge of Neckband to left V-neck edge, overlapping the V-neck bands.

Weave in all ends, wash, and block to diagram.

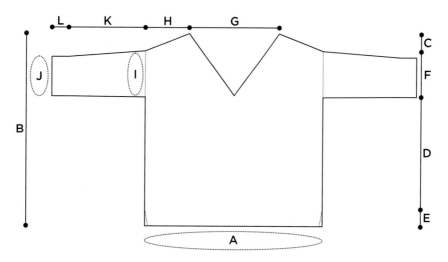

A 38 (42, 45.75, 49.5, 53.25, 57.25, 61)"
B 22 (22.25, 22.75, 24, 24.75, 25.25, 26)"
C 2"
D 13 (13, 13, 14, 14, 14, 14)"
E 2"
F 5 (5.25, 5.75, 6, 6.75, 7.25, 8)"
G 8.75 (10.75, 11, 11.5, 12.5, 13, 13)" (before ribbed neckband)
H 5.5 (5.5, 6, 6.75, 7.25, 8, 9)"
I 10.25 (10.75, 11.75, 12.5, 13.75, 14.5, 16)"
J 9.25 (9.75, 10.75, 11, 12.5, 13.25, 14)"
K 9.25"
L 2"

EARRACH CARDIGAN

by Helen Metcalfe

FINISHED MEASUREMENTS

31 (35, 39, 43, 47, 51, 55, 59, 63)″ finished bust circumference, buttoned; meant to be worn with 2–4″ positive ease
Sample is 39″ size; model is 33.5″ bust

YARN

Simply Cotton™ (sport weight, 100% Organic Cotton; 164 yards/50g): Marshmallow 24757, 7 (8, 9, 9, 10, 11, 12, 13, 14) hanks

NEEDLES

US 2.5 (3mm) straight or circular needles (24–32″), or size to obtain gauge
US 3 (3.25mm) straight or circular needles (24–32″), or size to obtain gauge

NOTIONS

Yarn Needle
Scrap Yarn or Stitch Holder
8 (8, 9, 9, 9, 9, 10, 11, 11) Buttons, 0.75″ in diameter
Blocking Pins and/or Wires

GAUGE

24 sts and 33 rows = 4″ in Stockinette Stitch on larger needles, blocked
29 sts and 32 rows = 4″ in 1x1 Rib on smaller needles, blocked (note that this is approximate due to the amount of stretch in the ribbing)
9-st Slipped Eyelet Stitch Pattern panel = 1.25″ on larger needles, blocked
15-st Sleeve Panel Stitch Pattern = 2.5″ on larger needles, blocked
53-st Back Panel Stitch Pattern = 8.75″ on larger needles, blocked

For pattern support, contact hmetcalfe@hotmail.co.uk

Earrach Cardigan

Notes:

Named after the Irish word for spring, Earrach is a lightweight cardigan perfect for lengthening warmer days. Lace panels set in Stockinette Stitch create interest in an otherwise simple garment.

The body is worked flat in one piece from the bottom up, then fronts and back are split and worked separately. Sleeves are worked flat. Neckband and button bands are picked up separately to finish.

Charts are worked flat; read RS rows (odd numbers) from right to left, and WS rows (even numbers) from left to right.

SE (slipped eyelet)
Sl3 to RH needle, pass first slipped st over second and third slipped sts. Sl the 2 remaining sts back to LH needle. K1, YO, K1.

Slipped Eyelet Stitch Pattern (flat over 9 sts)
Row 1 (RS): P1, K7, P1.
Row 2 (WS): K1, P7, K1.
Row 3: (P1, SE) two times, P1.
Row 4: (K1, P3) two times, K1.
Rep Rows 1–4 for pattern.

Back Panel Stitch Pattern (flat over 53 sts)
Row 1 (RS): (P1, K7, P1, K3, K2tog, YO, K3, YO, SSK, K3) two times, P1, K7, P1.
Row 2 (WS): K1, P7, K1, (P13, K1, P7, K1) two times.
Row 3: *(P1, SE) two times, P1, K2, K2tog, YO, K5, YO, SSK, K2; rep from * once more, (P1, SE) two times, P1.
Row 4: (K1, P3) two times, K1, *P13, (K1, P3) two times, K1; rep from * once more.
Row 5: (P1, K7, P1, K1, K2tog, YO, K2, P3, K2, YO, SSK, K1) two times, P1, K7, P1.
Row 6: K1, P7, K1, (P5, K3, P5, K1, P7, K1) two times.
Row 7: *(P1, SE) two times, P1, K2tog, YO, K3, P3, K3, YO, SSK; rep from * once more, (P1, SE) two times, P1.
Row 8: Rep Row 4.
Rep Rows 1–8 for pattern.

Sleeve Panel Stitch Pattern (flat over 15 sts)
Row 1 (RS): P1, K3, K2tog, YO, K3, YO, SSK, K3, P1.
Row 2 (WS): K1, P13, K1.
Row 3: P1, K2, K2tog, YO, K5, YO, SSK, K2, P1.
Row 4: Rep Row 2.
Row 5: P1, K1, K2tog, YO, K2, P3, K2, YO, SSK, K1, P1.
Row 6: K1, P5, K3, P5, K1.
Row 7: P1, K2tog, YO, K3, P3, K3, YO, SSK, P1.
Row 8: Rep Row 2.
Rep Rows 1–8 for pattern.

One Row Buttonhole (worked over 4 sts)
Bring yarn to front between needles, Sl next st P-wise and bring yarn to back between needles, wrapping base of st. (Sl next st P-wise and pass first slipped st over) three times. Sl st remaining on RH needle to LH needle and turn work. With WS facing, Cable CO 4 sts. Before placing last CO st onto LH needle, bring yarn to front between needles; place st on LH needle and turn work. Sl next st K-wise and pass last CO st over it.

DIRECTIONS
Using smaller needles, CO 225 (253, 283, 311, 341, 369, 399, 427, 457) sts.

Ribbed Body Hem
Row 1 (RS): (K1, P1) to last st, K1.
Row 2 (WS): (P1, K1) to last st, P1.
Rep Rows 1–2 until Body measures 1.5″ from CO edge, ending after a RS row.
Next Row (WS): Work 1x1 Rib as established for 7 (9, 5, 7, 5, 7, 3, 5, 3) sts, (K2tog, work Rib for 4 sts) until 8 (10, 8, 10, 6, 8, 6, 8, 4) sts remain, K2tog, work Rib to end. 189 (213, 237, 261, 285, 309, 333, 357, 381) sts.

Body
Change to larger needles.
Row 1 (RS): K4, work Row 1 of Slipped Eyelet Pattern, K55 (67, 79, 91, 103, 115, 127, 139, 151), work Row 1 of Back Panel Pattern, K55 (67, 79, 91, 103, 115, 127, 139, 151), work Row 1 of Slipped Eyelet Pattern, K4.
Row 2 (WS): P4, work Row 2 of Slipped Eyelet Pattern, P55 (67, 79, 91, 103, 115, 127, 139, 151), work Row 2 of Back Panel Pattern, P55 (67, 79, 91, 103, 115, 127, 139, 151), work Row 2 of Slipped Eyelet Pattern, P4.
Cont as established until piece measures 14.25 (14.25, 14.25, 15, 15, 15, 16.5, 16.5, 16.5)″ ending after a WS row.

Right Front
Maintain pattern for 46 (52, 58, 64, 70, 76, 82, 88, 94) sts, turn, now working these sts only, leaving remaining 143 (161, 179, 197, 215, 233, 251, 269, 287) sts on hold.
Cont as established and BO 3 (4, 4, 5, 5, 6, 7, 7, 8) sts at beginning of next WS row, then BO 2 (3, 3, 4, 4, 5, 6, 6, 7) sts at beginning of next WS row. 41 (45, 51, 55, 61, 65, 75, 79) sts.

Sizes - (35, 39, 43, 47, 51, 55, 59, 63)″ Only
Cont as established and BO - (2, 2, 3, 3, 4, 5, 5, 6) sts at beginning of next WS row. - (43, 49, 52, 58, 61, 64, 70, 73) sts.

Sizes - (-, -, 43, 47, 51, 55, 59, 63)″ Only
Cont as established and BO - (-, -, 2, 2, 3, 4, 4, 5) sts at beginning of next WS row. - (-, -, 50, 56, 58, 60, 66, 68) sts.

Sizes - (-, -, -, -, 51, 55, 59, 63)″ Only
Cont as established and BO - (-, -, -, -, 2, 3, 3, 4) sts at beginning of next WS row. - (-, -, -, -, 56, 57, 63, 64) sts.

Sizes - (-, -, -, -, -, 55, 59, 63)" Only
Cont as established and BO - (-, -, -, -, -, 2, 2, 3) sts at beginning of next WS row. - (-, -, -, -, -, 55, 61, 61) sts.

Size 63" Only
Cont as established and BO 2 sts at beginning of next WS row. 59 sts.

Resume All Sizes
Row 1 (RS): Work to last 3 sts, K2tog, K1. 1 st dec.
Row 2 (WS): WE.
Rep Rows 1–2 2 (2, 5, 3, 6, 3, 2, 5, 3) more times. 38 (40, 43, 46, 49, 52, 52, 55, 55) sts.

WE without shaping until Right Front measures 19.25 (19.5, 20.25, 21.5, 21.75, 22.5, 24.5, 25, 25.5)" from CO edge, ending after a WS row.
Next Row (RS): BO 11 (12, 12, 13, 14, 14, 14, 15, 15) sts, work to end. 27 (28, 31, 33, 35, 38, 38, 40, 40) sts.
Next Row and following WS rows: WE.
Cont as established and BO 3 sts at beginning of next 1 (1, 2, 2, 2, 2, 2, 2, 2) RS rows. 24 (25, 25, 27, 29, 32, 32, 34, 34) sts.
BO 2 sts at beginning of next 1 (1, 1, 1, 1, 1, 1, 2, 2) RS rows. 22 (23, 23, 25, 27, 30, 30, 30, 30) sts.
Next RS Row: K1, SSK, K to end. 1 st dec.
Rep last RS row 4 (4, 3, 3, 3, 3, 3, 2, 2) more times. 17 (18, 19, 21, 23, 26, 26, 27, 27) sts.
Cont as established and BO 3 (3, 3, 4, 4, 5, 5, 5, 5) sts at beginning of next 3 (2, 1, 4, 2, 4, 4, 3, 3) WS rows, then BO 4 (4, 4, 5, 5, 6, 6, 6, 6) sts at beginning of next 2 (3, 4, 1, 3, 1, 1, 2, 2) WS rows. 0 sts.

Back
Return 97 (109, 121, 133, 145, 157, 169, 181, 193) back sts to working needles, leaving 46 (52, 58, 64, 70, 76, 82, 88, 94) left sts on hold.
Cont as established, BO 3 (4, 4, 5, 5, 6, 7, 7, 8) sts at beginning of next 2 rows, then BO 2 (3, 3, 4, 4, 5, 6, 6, 7) sts at beginning of next 2 rows. 87 (95, 107, 115, 127, 135, 143, 155, 163) sts.

Sizes - (35, 39, 43, 47, 51, 55, 59, 63)" Only
Cont as established and BO - (2, 2, 3, 3, 4, 5, 5, 6) sts at beginning of next 2 rows. - (91, 103, 109, 121, 127, 133, 145, 151) sts.

Sizes - (-, -, 43, 47, 51, 55, 59, 63)" Only
Cont as established and BO - (-, -, 2, 2, 3, 4, 4, 5) sts at beginning of next 2 rows. - (-, -, 105, 117, 121, 125, 137, 141) sts.

Sizes - (-, -, -, -, 51, 55, 59, 63)" Only
Cont as established and BO - (-, -, -, -, 2, 3, 3, 4) sts at beginning of next 2 rows. - (-, -, -, -, 117, 119, 131, 133) sts

Sizes - (-, -, -, -, -, 55, 59, 63)" Only
Cont as established and - (-, -, -, -, -, 2, 2, 3) sts at beginning of next 2 rows. - (-, -, -, -, -, 115, 127, 127) sts.

Size 64" Only
Cont as established and BO 2 sts at beginning of next 2 rows. 123 sts.

Resume All Sizes
Row 1 (RS): K1, SSK, maintain pattern to last 3 sts, K2tog, K1. 2 sts dec.
Row 2 (WS): WE.
Rep Rows 1–2 2 (2, 5, 3, 6, 3, 2, 5, 3) more times. 81 (85, 91, 97, 103, 109, 109, 115, 115) sts.
Cont without shaping until work measures 21.25 (21.5, 22.25, 23.5, 23.75, 24.5, 26.5, 27, 27.5)" from CO edge, ending after a WS row.
Cont as established and BO 3 (3, 3, 4, 4, 5, 5, 5, 5) sts at beginning of next 6 (4, 2, 8, 4, 8, 8, 6, 6) rows, then BO 4 (4, 4, 5, 5, 6, 6, 6, 6) sts at beginning of next 4 (6, 8, 2, 6, 2, 2, 4, 4) rows. 47 (49, 53, 55, 57, 57, 57, 61, 61) sts.
Place remaining sts on a st holder or scrap yarn.

Left Front
Return 46 (52, 58, 64, 70, 76, 82, 88, 94) sts to working needles with RS facing.
BO 3 (4, 4, 5, 5, 6, 7, 7, 8) sts, work to end of row.
Cont as established and BO 2 (3, 3, 4, 4, 5, 6, 6, 7) sts at beginning of next RS row. 41 (45, 51, 55, 61, 65, 69, 75, 79) sts.

Sizes - (35, 39, 43, 47, 51, 55, 59, 63)" Only
Cont as established and BO - (2, 2, 3, 3, 4, 5, 5, 6) sts at beginning of next RS row. - (43, 49, 52, 58, 61, 64, 70, 73) sts.

Sizes - (-, -, 43, 47, 51, 55, 59, 63)" Only
Cont as established and BO - (-, -, 2, 2, 3, 4, 4, 5) sts at beginning of next RS row. - (-, -, 50, 56, 58, 60, 66, 68) sts.

Sizes - (-, -, -, -, 51, 55, 59, 63)" Only
Cont as established and BO - (-, -, -, -, 2, 3, 3, 4) sts at beginning of next RS row. - (-, -, -, -, 56, 57, 63, 64) sts.

Sizes - (-, -, -, - -, 55, 59, 63)" Only
Cont as established and BO - (-, -, -, -, -, 2, 2, 3) sts at beginning of next RS row. - (-, -, -, -, -, 55, 61, 61) sts.

Size 64" Only
Cont as established and BO 2 sts at beginning of next RS row. 59 sts.

Resume All Sizes
Row 1 (RS): K1, SSK, work to end. 1 st dec.
Row 2 (WS): WE.
Rep Rows 1–2 2 (2, 5, 3, 6, 3, 2, 5, 3) more times. 38 (40, 43, 46, 49, 52, 52, 55, 55) sts.
WE until work measures 19.25 (19.5, 20.25, 21.5, 21.75, 22.5, 24.5, 25, 25.5)" ending after a WS row.
Next Row (RS): WE.
Next Row (WS): BO 11 (12, 12, 13, 14, 14, 14, 15, 15) sts, work to end. 27 (28, 31, 33, 35, 38, 38, 40, 40) sts.
Cont as established and BO 3 sts at beginning of next 1 (1, 2, 2, 2, 2, 2, 2, 2) WS rows, then BO 2 sts at beginning of next 1 (1, 1, 1, 1, 1, 1, 2, 2) WS rows. 22 (23, 23, 25, 27, 30, 30, 30, 30) sts.
Dec Row (RS): Work to last 3 sts, K2tog, K1. 1 st dec.
Rep Dec Row 4 (4, 3, 3, 3, 3, 3, 2, 2) more times. 17 (18, 19, 21, 23, 26, 26, 27, 27) sts.

Cont as established and BO 3 (3, 3, 4, 4, 5, 5, 5, 5) sts at beginning of next 3 (2, 1, 4, 2, 4, 4, 3, 3) RS rows, then BO 4 (4, 4, 5, 5, 6, 6, 6, 6) sts at beginning of next 2 (3, 4, 1, 3, 1, 1, 2, 2) RS rows. 0 sts.

Sleeves (make two the same)

Ribbed Cuff

Using smaller needles, loosely CO 61 (63, 69, 75, 77, 77, 81, 81, 83) sts.

Row 1 (RS): (K1, P1) to last st, K1.
Row 2 (WS): (P1, K1) to last st, P1.
Rep Rows 1–2 until Sleeve measures 1.5" from CO edge, ending after a RS row.
Next Row: Work Rib as established for 3 (3, 7, 5, 5, 5, 7, 7, 9) sts, *K2tog, work Rib for 4 (4, 4, 3, 4, 4, 3, 3, 3) sts; rep from * to last 4 (6, 8, 5, 6, 6, 9, 9, 9) sts, K2tog, work Rib to end. 51 (53, 59, 61, 65, 65, 67, 67, 69) sts.

Change to larger needles.
Row 1 (RS): K18 (19, 22, 23, 25, 25, 26, 26, 27), work Row 1 of Sleeve Panel Pattern, K to end.
Row 2 (WS): P18 (19, 22, 23, 25, 25, 26, 26, 27), work Row 2 of Sleeve Panel Pattern, P to end.

Inc Row (RS): K1, M1, work to last st, M1, K1. 2 sts inc.
WE for 13 (13, 13, 11, 9, 9, 5, 5, 3) rows.
Rep previous 14 (14, 14, 12, 10, 10, 6, 6, 4) rows 4 (4, 4, 10, 13, 13, 22, 13, 14) more times. 61 (63, 69, 83, 93, 93, 113, 95, 99) sts.

Sizes 31 (35, 39, -, -, -, -, 59, 63)" Only

Work Inc Row.
WE for 11 (11, 11, -, -, -, -, 3, 5) rows.
Rep previous 12 (12, 12, -, -, -, -, 4, 6) rows 5 (5, 5, -, -, -, -, 14, 15) more times. 71 (73, 79, -, -, -, -, 123, 129) sts.

Resume All Sizes

Cont without shaping until work measures 19.5 (20, 20, 20.5, 20.5, 21, 21, 21.5, 21.5)" from CO edge, ending after a WS row.
BO 3 (4, 4, 5, 5, 6, 7, 7, 8) sts at beginning of next 2 rows. 65 (65, 71, 73, 83, 81, 99, 109, 113) sts.
Work 2 (0, 2, 2, 0, 0, 0, 0, 0) rows without shaping.

Dec Row (RS): K1, SSK, work to last 3 sts, K2tog, K1. 2 sts dec.
Rep Dec Row every RS row 6 (17, 19, 20, 5, 23, 2, 0, 1) more times. 51 (29, 31, 31, 71, 33, 93, 107, 109) sts.

Sizes 31 (-, -, -, 47, -, 55, 59, 63)" Only

Work one WS row. Rep RS Dec Row once more. 49 (-, -, -, 69, -, 91, 105, 107) sts.
Dec Row (WS): P1, SSP, P to last 3 sts, P2tog, P1. 2 sts dec.
*Rep RS Dec Row every RS Row 7 (-, -, -, 6, -, 3, 1, 2) times.
Work RS Dec Row once more, then work WS Dec Row once; Rep from * - (-, -, -, -, -, 4, 7, 6) more times. 29 (-, -, -, 51, -, 39, 55, 49) sts.
Cont working RS Dec Row every RS row 0 (-, -, -, 9, -, 0, 7, 3) more times. 29 (-, -, -, 33, -, 39, 41, 43) sts.

Resume All Sizes

Starting with a RS row, BO 3 sts at beginning of next 4 rows. 17 (17, 19, 19, 21, 21, 27, 29, 31) sts.
BO remaining sts.

Neckband

Sew shoulder seams.

With smaller needles and RS facing, starting with top right edge, PU and K 32 (33, 34, 35, 36, 36, 36, 37, 37) sts evenly around right front neck, K47 (49, 53, 55, 57, 57, 57, 61, 61) sts from back neck, PU and K 32 (33, 34, 35, 36, 36, 36, 37, 37) sts evenly around left front neck. 111 (115, 121, 125, 129, 129, 129, 135, 135) sts.

Row 1 (WS): (P1, K1) to last st, P1.
Row 2 (RS): (K1, P1) to last st, K1.
Rep Rows 1–2 three more times, then Row 1 once more.
BO all sts.

Left Button Band

With smaller needles and with RS facing, starting at neckband edge of Left Front, PU and K 131 (133, 139, 147, 149, 153, 165, 169, 173) sts.

Row 1 (WS): (P1, K1) to last st, P1.
Row 2 (RS): (K1, P1) to last st, K1.
Rep Rows 1–2 three more times.
BO all sts.

Right Buttonhole Band

With smaller needles and with RS facing, starting at lower edge of Right Front, PU and K 131 (133, 139, 147, 149, 153, 165, 169, 173) sts.

Row 1 (WS): (P1, K1) to last st, P1.
Row 2 (RS): (K1, P1) to last st, K1.
Rep Row 1 once more.
Next Row (RS): Work Rib for 4 (5, 3, 3, 4, 2, 4, 2, 4) sts, *work One Row Buttonhole, work Rib for 13 (13, 12, 13, 13, 14, 13, 12, 12) sts; rep from * to last 8 (9, 8, 8, 9, 7, 8, 7, 9) sts, work One Row Buttonhole, work Rib to end.
Rep Rows 1–2 two more times.
BO all sts.

Finishing

Line up center of sleeve head with shoulder seam, sew seams using Mattress Stitch. Sew sleeve seam.
Rep for other sleeve.
Attach buttons along left button band to line up with buttonholes.
Weave in ends, wash, and block to diagram.

Earrach Chart

Sleeve Panel Pattern   **Slipped Eyelet Pattern**

	31	30	29	28	27	26	25	24	23	22	21	20	19	18	17	16	15	14	13	12	11	10	9	8	7	6	5	4	3	2	1	
8	●				●				●														●			●					●	
	●	├─O─┤		●		├─O─┤		●		＼	O				●	●	●				O	／	●	├─O─┤		●		├─O─┤		●	7
6	●								●							●	●	●					●								●	
	●				●				●			＼	O			●	●	●		O	／		●								●	5
4	●				●				●														●			●					●	
	●	├─O─┤		●		├─O─┤		●			＼	O						O	／			●	├─O─┤		●		├─O─┤		●	3
2	●								●														●								●	
	●								●		＼	O					O	／					●								●	1

Back Panel Pattern is all sts
with boxed rep worked twice.

LEGEND

K
RS: Knit stitch
WS: Purl stitch

P
● RS: Purl stitch
WS: Knit stitch

YO
O Yarn over

K2tog
Knit 2 stitches together as one stitch

SSK
Slip, slip, knit slipped stitches together

Slipped Eyelet (SE)
Sl3 to RH needle, pass first slipped stitch over second and third slipped stitches, slip the 2 remaining stitches back to LH needle; K1, YO, K1.

Back Panel Pattern Repeat
Repeat two times for Back Panel (then work to end of chart)

Slipped Eyelet Pattern
Work only these 9 stitches when directed to work Slipped Eyelet Pattern

Sleeve Panel Pattern
Work only these 15 stitches when directed to work Sleeve Panel Pattern

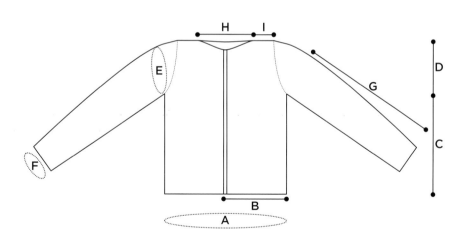

A   32 (36, 40, 44, 48, 52, 56, 60, 64)"
B   8.25 (9.25, 10.25, 11.25, 12.25, 13.25, 14.25, 15.25, 16.25)"
C   14.25 (14.25, 14.25, 15, 15, 15, 16.5, 16.5, 16.5)"
D   7 (7.25, 8, 8.5, 8.75, 9.5, 10, 10.5, 11)"
E   11.75 (12, 13, 13.75, 15.25, 15.25, 18.75, 20.5, 21.5)"
F   8.5 (8.75, 9.75, 10.25, 10.75, 10.75, 11.25, 11.25, 11.5)"
G   19.5 (20, 20, 20.5, 20.5, 21, 21, 21.5, 21.5)"
H   7.75 (8.25, 8.75, 9.25, 9.5, 9.5, 9.5, 10.25, 10.25)"
I   2.75 (3, 3.25, 3.5, 3.75, 4.25, 4.25, 4.5, 4.5)"

ELEMENTS SWEATER

by Fiona Munro

FINISHED MEASUREMENTS

32 (36, 40, 44, 48, 52, 56, 60, 64)"
finished bust circumference; meant
to be worn with 2–4" positive ease
Sample is 40" size; model is 33.5" bust

YARN

Shine™ (worsted weight, 60% Pima
Cotton, 40% Modal® natural beech wood
fiber; 75 yards/50g): Hydrangea 25351,
14 (15, 16, 17, 18, 19, 20, 21, 22) skeins

NEEDLES

US 6 (4mm) 24–32" circular needles,
and DPNs, or size to obtain gauge

NOTIONS

Yarn Needle
Stitch Markers
Stitch Holder or Scrap Yarn
Blocking Pins and/or Wires

GAUGE

20 sts and 28 rnds = 4" in Cable Lace
Pattern, Stockinette Stitch, and Seed
Stitch, all in the round, blocked

For pattern support, contact munrosisters3@gmail.com

Elements Sweater

Notes:

The Elements Sweater is a gorgeous lace pullover, perfect for all seasons with its comfortable loose fit and modern lace detail inspired by knitted cable work.

The sweater is worked mainly in the round from the bottom up with the lace detail worked over the front and back of the body, and a small lace faux cable up each sleeve.

Charts are worked both in the round and flat; only odd numbered rounds, or RS rows, are shown on charts—read all chart rows from right to left. For bottom of the Body and the Sleeves (in the round), even numbered rounds (not shown) are knit plain. For top of the Front and Back sections (where armholes are worked), charts are worked flat with WS rows (even numbers, not shown) purled plain.

Seed Stitch (in the round over an even number of sts)
Rnd 1: (K1, P1) to end.
Rnd 2: (P1, K1) to end.
Rep Rnds 1-2 for pattern.

DIRECTIONS

Body
Loosely CO 160 (180, 200, 220, 240, 260, 280, 300, 320) sts with circular needles. Join to work in the rnd, being careful not to twist sts; PM for BOR.
Work Seed Stitch until piece measures 2" from CO edge.

Setup Rnd: K2 (7, 12, 17, 22, 27, 32, 37, 42), PM, K76, PM, K2 (7, 12, 17, 22, 27, 32, 37, 42), PM, K2 (7, 12, 17, 22, 27, 32, 37, 42), PM, K76, PM, K2 (7, 12, 17, 22, 27, 32, 37, 42).
Next Rnd: K to M, SM, work Small Cable Chart once, work Large Cable Chart two times, work Small Cable Chart once, SM, K2 (7, 12, 17, 22, 27, 32, 37, 42), SM, K2 (7, 12, 17, 22, 27, 32, 37, 42), SM, work Small Cable Chart once, work Large Cable Chart two times, work Small Cable Chart once, SM, K to end.

Cont as established until piece measures 16 (16, 16.5, 16.5, 17, 17, 17.5, 17.5, 18)" from CO edge.

Divide for Front and Back
Place first 80 (90, 100, 110, 120, 130, 140, 150, 160) sts worked on st holder or scrap yarn for front.

Back
Cont as established flat until armhole measures 7.5 (8, 8, 8.5, 8.5, 9, 9, 9.5, 9.5)".
BO all sts.

Front
Cont as established flat until armhole measures 3.5 (4, 4, 4.5, 4.5, 5, 5, 5.5, 5.5)" ending with a WS row. Place center 28 (28, 28, 28, 28, 28, 28, 28, 28) sts on a st holder or scrap yarn.

Front Right & Left
Work Front Right and Front Left separately at the same time. Cont as established, decreasing 1 st at neck edge (K2tog on RS or P2tog on WS) every row 3 (3, 4, 4, 5, 5, 6, 6, 7) times. 23 (28, 32, 37, 41, 46, 50, 55, 59) sts each side.
Cont as established, decreasing 1 st at neck edge (K2tog on RS or P2tog on WS) every other row three times. 20 (25, 29, 34, 38, 43, 47, 52, 56) sts each side.
Cont as established until armhole measures 7.5 (8, 8, 8.5, 8.5, 9, 9, 9.5, 9.5)". To maintain the Large Cable Chart sts, over the 5 (5, 4, 4, 3, 3, 2, 2, 1) sts, K1 rather than K2tog or SSK if there is no YO beside the dec st in order to maintain the number of Large Cable Chart sts.
BO all sts.

Sleeves (make two the same)
Loosely CO 43 (45, 49, 51, 53, 55, 57, 57, 59) sts with DPNs. Join to work in the rnd, being careful not to twist sts; PM for BOR.
Work Seed Stitch until piece measures 2" from CO edge.

Setup Rnd: K15 (16, 18, 19, 20, 21, 22, 22, 23), PM, K13, PM, K15 (16, 18, 19, 20, 21, 22, 22, 23).
Next Rnd: K to M, SM, work Small Cable Chart once, SM, K to end.
Inc Rnd: K1, M1, K to M, SM, work Small Cable Chart once, SM, K to last st, M1, K1. 2 sts inc.

Cont as established and work Inc Rnd every five rnds a total of 16 (18, 16, 17, 16, 18, 17, 19, 18) times. 75 (81, 81, 85, 85, 91, 91, 95, 95) sts.
Cont as established until piece measures 18 (18.5, 18.5, 19, 19, 19.5, 19.5, 20, 20)" from CO edge.
BO all sts.

Neckband
Sew shoulder seams and sleeves to body.

PU and K 40 (40, 42, 42, 44, 44, 46, 46, 48) sts with DPNs along Back neck edge, PU and K 20 (20, 21, 21, 22, 22, 23, 23, 24) sts from side Front neck edge, place 28 held sts on needles, and PU and K 20 (20, 21, 21, 22, 22, 23, 23, 24) sts along other Front neck edge. 108 (108, 112, 112, 116, 116, 120, 120, 124) sts total. Join to work in the rnd.
Work Seed Stitch until neckband measures 1".
BO all sts.

Finishing
Weave in ends, wash, and block to diagram.

Large Cable Chart

25	24	23	22	21	20	19	18	17	16	15	14	13	12	11	10	9	8	7	6	5	4	3	2	1	
\	O	B	\		O	B	\		O	B				B	O	/		B	O	/	B	O	/		15
\	O	B	\		O	B	\		O	B				B	O	/		B	O	/	B	O	/		13
		O	B	\		O	B	\		O	B		B	O	/		B	O	/		B	O	/	\	11
\		O		O	B	\		O	B			B	O	/		B	O	/		B	O	/			9
\	O	B	\		O	B	\		O	B				B	O	/		B	O	/	B	O	/		7
\	O	B	\		O	B	\		O	B				B	O	/		B	O	/	B	O	/		5
		O	B	\		O	B	\		O	B		B	O	/		B	O	/		B	O	/	\	3
\		O		O	B	\		O	B			B	O	/		B	O	/		B	O	/			1

Small Cable Chart

13	12	11	10	9	8	7	6	5	4	3	2	1	
	\	O	B						B	O	/		15
		\	O	B				B	O	/			13
			\	O	B		B	O	/				11
				\	O	B	O	/					9
					O	B	O						7
				B	O	λ	O	B					5
		B	O	/				O	B				3
	B	O	/						O	B			1

LEGEND

	Knit Stitch
B	**K TBL** — Knit stitch through the back loop
O	**YO** — Yarn over
/	**K2tog** — Knit 2 stitches together as one stitch
\	**SSK** — Slip, slip, knit slipped stitches together
λ	**SK2P** — Slip 1 knit-wise, K2tog, pass slip stitch over K2tog

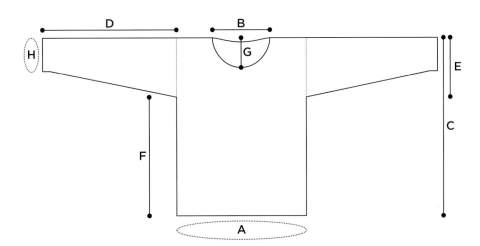

A 32 (36, 40, 44, 48, 52, 56, 60, 64)"
B 8 (8, 8.5, 8.5, 9, 9, 9.25, 9.25, 9.5)"
C 23.5 (24, 24.5, 25, 25.5, 26, 26.5, 27, 27.5)"
D 18 (18.5, 18.5, 19, 19, 19.5, 19.5, 20, 20)"
E 7.5 (8, 8, 8.5, 8.5, 9, 9, 9.5, 9.5)"
F 16 (16, 16.5, 16.5, 17, 17, 17.5, 17.5, 18)"
G 4 (4, 4, 4, 4, 4, 4, 4, 4)"
H 8.5 (9, 10, 10, 10.5, 11, 11.5, 11.5, 12)"

FLOCKING COWL

by Lee Meredith

FINISHED MEASUREMENTS

25–26 (31–32.5)" circumference × 9–9.5 (11.5–12)" height, for Aran-bulky weight
1-color sample is larger size, 2-color sample is smaller size

YARN

Snuggle Puff™ (Aran/heavy worsted weight, 70% Pima Cotton, 30% Nylon; 142 yards/50g): Polliwog 27814, 2 balls
or
Billow™ (bulky weight, 100% Pima Cotton; 120 yards/100g): MC Tempest 28028, 1 (2) hanks; CC Celadon 28021, 1 hank

NEEDLES

US 10.5 (6.5mm) 16" circular needles, or size to obtain gauge

NOTIONS

Yarn Needle
Stitch Marker

GAUGE

12 sts and 30 rnds = 4" in Flocking Pattern in the round, blocked without stretching (gauge is approximate and not crucial, but it will affect finished size and yardage requirements)

For pattern support, contact leemeredith@gmail.com

Flocking Cowl

Notes:

This fun, easy-to-memorize stitch pattern creates a very squishy, textured fabric; a great effect for a cotton yarn, which can tend to be a bit, well, unsquishy. The Garter Stitch base features slipped strands of yarn pulled up over several rows, literally squishing the fabric together with a V motif, vaguely resembling a flock of birds flying together (or flocking) over a cloudy sky.

Make a lighter weight, airier cowl with the heavy worsted weight Snuggle Puff yarn, which fluffs to look full but feels feather-light to wear. Or make a more substantial piece in the heavier weight Billow cotton, still cool for transitional weather but with a bit more heft. While using the same needle size with the two yarns will result in very similar gauges to each other, the density of fabric will differ, and the sizes may vary slightly, hence the size ranges given, Snuggle Puff on the smaller end of the scale, and Billow on the larger.

Follow the MC/CC instructions for the two-color version; if making a single color version, simply ignore the MC/CC and make the whole cowl in one color.

Note that you may choose to make a two-color version in Snuggle Puff, or a one-color version in Billow. You may also choose to go off-book with your sizing, if you like a longer/shorter/wider cowl—cast on any multiple of ten stitches, and work any number of stitch pattern repeats before working the final rounds.

Chart is worked in the round; read each chart row from right to left as a RS row.

Purl-wise Decrease Bind Off
*P2tog, Sl just-worked st to LH needle without twisting; rep from * until all sts are bound off.

Sl5 WYIF (slip 5 with yarn in front)
Sl 5 sts WYIF and carried very loosely. When working the following st, spread the 5 sts out on RH needle to be sure yarn is loose across them (it should be the length of the 5 sts spread out comfortably on needle, not much longer).

KU3 (knit under three strands)
Insert RH needle under the three previously carried strands of yarn, then through st, and knit the st, then bring needle back under and out from the strands.

LEGEND

	Main Color		●	Purl Stitch
	Contrasting Color (optional)		V̲	Sl WYIF — Slip stitch purl-wise, with yarn in front
	Knit Stitch		🁢	KU3 — Knit under 3 strands (see *Notes*)

Flocking Pattern (in the round over a multiple of 10 sts)
Rnd 1 (MC): K all.
Rnd 2 (MC): P all.
Rnd 3 (MC): K all.
Rnd 4 (CC): (P5, Sl5 WYIF) to end.
Rnd 5 (CC): (K2, KU3, K2, Sl5 WYIF) to end.
Rnd 6 (CC): (P5, Sl5 WYIF) to end.
Rnd 7 (MC): K all.
Rnd 8 (MC): P all.
Rnd 9 (MC): K all.
Rnd 10 (CC): (Sl5 WYIF, P5) to end.
Rnd 11 (CC): (Sl5 WYIF, K2, KU3, K2) to end.
Rnd 12 (CC): (Sl5 WYIF, P5) to end.
Rep Rnds 1–12 for pattern.

DIRECTIONS
With MC, CO 80 (100) sts. Join in the rnd, being careful not to twist sts; PM for BOR.
Purl one rnd.

Work Flocking Pattern from chart or written instructions around eight (ten) times, starting with Rnd 1. On first rep, work Rnd 5 St 3 as a K st (instead of KU3).
Work five (seven) total reps of Flocking Pattern Rnds 1–12.

Work Rnds 1–3 of Flocking Pattern once more, then work as follows.
Ending Rnd 1 (CC): P all.
Ending Rnd 2 (CC): (K2, KU3, K7) to end.
Ending Rnd 3 (CC): P all.
Ending Rnd 4 (MC): K all.
Ending Rnds 5–6 (MC): Rep Rnds 3–4 once more (all in MC).
BO P-wise, with MC, loosely, using the Purl-wise Decrease Bind Off.

Finishing
Weave in ends. Wash and block as desired; hand washing and laying flat to dry is recommended—to retain squishy texture, do not stretch when blocking. Lay flat, smooshed in a bit, both lengthwise and widthwise, changing position a couple of times per day as it dries, to dry thoroughly and avoid creases.

Flocking Pattern

10	9	8	7	6	5	4	3	2	1	
●	●	●	●	●	V	V	V	V	V	12
		🁢			V	V	V	V	V	11
●	●	●	●	●	V	V	V	V	V	10
										9
●	●	●	●	●	●	●	●	●	●	8
										7
V	V	V	V	V	●	●	●	●	●	6
V	V	V	V	V			🁢			5
V	V	V	V	V	●	●	●	●	●	4
										3
●	●	●	●	●	●	●	●	●	●	2
										1

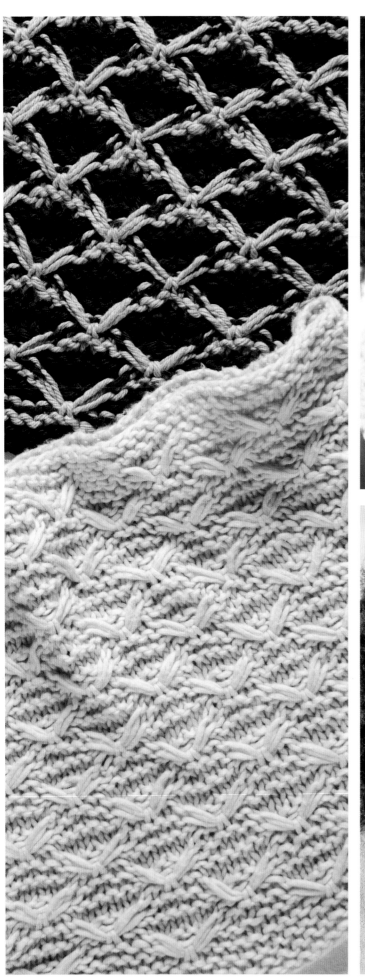

GIRLS JUST WANNA HAVE SUN TOP

by Jessy Pellett

FINISHED MEASUREMENTS

38.25 (42.75, 46.75, 50.75, 54.75, 58.75)"
finished bust circumference; meant to
be worn with 4–6" positive ease
Sample is 38.25" size; model is 33.5" bust

YARN

Comfy™ Color Mist (worsted weight,
75% Pima Cotton, 25% Acrylic; 219
yards/100g): MC Notebook 28079, 2 (3,
3, 3, 3, 3) hanks; CC Bare 28081, 2 (2, 2,
2, 3, 3) hanks

NEEDLES

US 8 (5mm) 32" circular needles, or size
to obtain gauge

US 6 (4mm) 32" circular needles,
or two sizes smaller than size used
to obtain gauge

NOTIONS

Yarn Needle
Stitch Markers
Scrap Yarn or Stitch Holder
Blocking Pins and/or Wires

GAUGE

18 sts and 25 rnds = 4" in Stockinette
Stitch in the round, blocked
17 sts and 26 rows = 4" in Lace Rays
Chart pattern, blocked

For pattern support, contact ThatMNYarnGirl@gmail.com

Girls Just Wanna Have Sun Top

Notes:

Spring sunshine is celebrated in this tee, with a beautiful lace motif shaped like the sun; its rays spread out over the back and wrap the shoulders in their warmth!

The top is worked from the bottom up with a Reverse Stockinette Stitch border. The Stockinette body is worked in the round with no side seaming required. The boxy design requires minimal shaping, and Kitchener Stitch is used to join it all together at the shoulders.

Charts are worked flat; read RS rows (odd numbers) from right to left, and WS rows (even numbers) from left to right.

DIRECTIONS

Hem

Front Hem (worked flat)
Using smaller needles and MC, CO 76 (86, 96, 105, 113, 122) sts. Work Rev St st for four rows, slipping first st of every row.
Row 5: Switch to larger needles. Sl1, K5 (5, 5, 5, 2, 1), *M1, K7 (8, 10, 11, 11, 12); rep from * 9 (9, 8, 8, 9, 9) more times. 86 (96, 105, 114, 123, 132) sts.
Work St st and cont to Sl first st of every row until front hem measures 4", ending on a WS row. Place sts on st holder or scrap yarn.

Back Hem
Work as for Front Hem, but do not place Back Hem sts on holder.

Body

Setup Rnd: PM for BOR, K all sts from st holder, then join with sts from Back Hem. 172 (192, 210, 228, 246, 264) sts.
Work St st around all sts for 59 (56, 54, 53, 51, 50) more rnds.

Fade
Rnd 1: Using CC, K all.
Rnd 2: Using MC, K all.
Rnd 3: Rep Rnd 2.
Rnds 4–13: Rep Rnds 1–2.
Rnd 14–15: Rep Rnd 1.
Rnd 16: Rep Rnd 2.
Rnd 17: Rep Rnd 1.

Divide for Yoke
K86 (96, 105, 114, 123, 132) for Front and place on st holder or scrap yarn, K to end; turn to begin working flat.

Top Back

Back of sweater is worked flat over remaining 86 (96, 105, 114, 123, 132) sts.
Switch to smaller needle.

Sizes 38.25 (-, -, 50.75, -, -)" Only
Setup Row (WS): Sl1, P2, M1, P to end. 87 (-, -, 115, -, -) sts.

Sizes - (42.75, -, -, -, 58.75)" Only
Setup Row (WS): Sl1, P2, P2tog, P to end. - (95, -, -, -, 131) sts.

Size 46.75" Only
Setup Row (WS): Sl1, P2, P2tog, P to last 5 sts, P2tog, P3. 103 sts.

Size 54.75" Only
Setup Row (WS): Sl1, P to end.

Resume All Sizes
Next Row (RS): Begin Sun Lace chart for indicated size. Work all rows of Sun Lace chart.
Work Lace Rays chart for indicated size 1 (2, 2, 3, 3, 3) time(s), then work first 6 (0, 4, 0, 2, 6) Lace Rays chart rows once more.

Back Neck
Right Side
Row 1 (RS): Sl1, K3 (2, 0, 0, 3, 1), *K2, K2tog, YO; rep from * 4 (6, 7, 9, 9, 10) more times, K4 (1, 3, 1, 2, 4). 28 (32, 36, 42, 46, 50) sts. Place remaining 59 (63, 67, 73, 77, 81) sts on st holder or scrap yarn.
Row 2 (WS): BO 1 st, P to end. 27 (31, 35, 41, 45, 49) sts.
Row 3: Sl1, K2 (1, 3, 3, 2, 0), *K2, K2tog, YO; rep from * 4 (6, 6, 8, 9, 10) more times, K4 (1, 3, 1, 2, 4).
Row 4: BO 1 st, P to end. 26 (30, 34, 40, 44, 48) sts.
Row 5: Sl1, K1 (0, 2, 2, 1, 3), *K2, K2tog, YO; rep from * 4 (6, 6, 8, 9, 9) more times, K4 (1, 3, 1, 2, 4).
Row 6: Sl1, P to end.
Place sts on st holder or scrap yarn.

Left Side
Return to remaining 59 (63, 67, 73, 77, 81) held sts. Keep 31 center sts on holder for back neck and place 28 (32, 36, 42, 46, 50) left sts onto working needles.
Row 1 (RS): K4 (1, 3, 1, 2, 4), *YO, SSK, K2; rep from * 4 (6, 7, 9, 9, 10) more times, K4 (3, 1, 1, 4, 2). 28 (32, 36, 42, 46, 50) sts.
Row 2 and all WS rows: Sl1, P to end.
Row 3: BO 1 st, K4 (1, 3, 1, 2, 4), *YO, SSK, K2; rep from * 4 (6, 6, 8, 9, 10) more times, K3 (2, 4, 4, 3, 1). 27 (31, 35, 41, 45, 49) sts.
Row 5: BO 1 st, K4 (1, 3, 1, 2, 4), *YO, SSK, K2; rep from * 4 (6, 6, 8, 9, 9) more times, K2 (1, 3, 3, 2, 4). 26 (30, 34, 40, 44, 48) sts.
Place sts on st holder or scrap yarn.

Top Front
Sizes 38.25 (-, -, 50.75, -, -)" Only
Setup Row (RS): Sl1, K2, M1, K to end. 87 (-, -, 115, -, -) sts.

Sizes - (42.75, -, -, -, 58.75)" Only
Setup Row (RS): Sl1, K2, K2tog, K to end. - (95, -, -, -, 131) sts.

Size 46.75" Only
Setup Row (RS): Sl1, K2, K2tog, K to last 5 sts, K2tog, K3. 103 sts.

Size 54.75" Only
Setup Row (RS): Sl1, K to end.

Resume All Sizes
Next Row (WS): P across.

Work Front Lace Rays chart for indicated size. Each time Row 1 is worked, an additional rep will be added to each side of sleeve lace detailing and the number of St sts will be reduced within body. If using a M, place it after last right side rep and before first left side rep. Ms will need to be moved over 2 sts on Rows 1 and 5 of chart.

Size 38.25": Work Front Lace Rays chart, starting on Row 7. Work chart four more times then work Rows 1–2 once more.
Size 42.75": Work Front Lace Rays chart five times.
Size 46.75": Work Front Lace Rays chart, starting on Row 3. Work chart four more times then work Rows 1–4 once more.
Size 50.75": Work Front Lace Rays chart, starting on Row 7. Work chart five more times then work Rows 1–4 once more.
Size 54.75": Work Front Lace Rays chart six times then work Rows 1–2 once more.
Size 58.75": Work Front Lace Rays chart, starting on Row 3. Work chart five more times then work Rows 1–6 once more.

Front Neck

Left Side
Row 1 (RS): Using smaller needles, Sl1, K1 (0, 2, 2, 1, 3), *K2, YO, SSK; rep from * 5 (6, 7, 8, 9, 10) more times, K9 (10, 8, 10, 11, 9), turn. 35 (39, 43, 49, 53, 57) sts. Place remaining 52 (56, 60, 66, 70, 74) sts on st holder or scrap yarn.
Row 2 (WS): BO 2 sts, P to end. 33 (37, 41, 47, 51, 55) sts.
Row 3: Sl1, K2 (1, 3, 3, 2, 0), *K2, YO, SSK; rep from * 5 (6, 7, 8, 9, 11) more times, K to end.
Row 4: BO 2 sts, P to end. 31 (35, 39, 45, 49, 53) sts.
Row 5: Sl1, K3 (2, 0, 0, 3, 1), *K2, YO, SSK; rep from * 5 (6, 8, 9, 9, 11) more times, K to end.
Row 6: BO 2 sts, P to end. 29 (33, 37, 43, 47, 51) sts.
Row 7: Sl1, K0 (3, 1, 1, 0, 2), *K2, YO, SSK; rep from * 6 (6, 7, 9, 10, 11) more times, K0, (1, 3, 1, 2, 0).
Row 8: BO 1 st, P to end. 28 (32, 36, 42, 46, 50) sts.
Row 9: Sl1, K1 (0, 2, 2, 1, 3), *K2, YO, SSK; rep from * 5 (6, 7, 8, 10, 10) more times, K2 (3, 1, 3, 0, 2).
Row 10: BO 1 st, P to end. 27 (31, 35, 41 45, 49) sts.
Row 11: Sl1, K2 (1, 3, 3, 2, 0), *K2, YO, SSK; rep from * 5 (6, 6, 8, 9, 11) more times, K0 (1, 3, 1, 2, 0).
Row 12: BO 1 st, P to end. 26 (30, 34, 40, 44, 48) sts.
Row 13: Sl1, K3 (2, 0, 0, 3, 1), *K2, YO, SSK; rep from * 4 (5, 7, 8, 9, 10) more times, K2 (3, 1, 3, 0, 2).
Row 14: Sl1, P to end.
Row 15: Sl1, K0 (3, 1, 1, 0, 2), *K2, YO, SSK; rep from * 5 (5, 7, 8, 9, 10) more times, K1 (2, 0, 2, 3, 1).
Row 16: Rep Row 14.
Row 17: Sl1, K1 (0, 2, 2, 1, 3), *K2, YO, SSK; rep from * 5 (6, 6, 8, 9, 10) more times, K0 (1, 3, 1, 2, 0).
Place remaining sts on holder.

Right Side
Return to remaining 52 (56, 60, 66, 70, 74) held sts. Keep 17 center sts on holder for base of neck and place 35 (39, 43, 49, 53, 57) right sts onto smaller needles.
Row 1 (RS): K9 (10, 8, 10, 11, 9), *K2tog, YO, K2; rep from * 5 (6, 7, 8, 9, 10) more times, K to end.
Row 2 and all WS rows: Sl1, P to end.

Row 3: BO 2 sts, K6 (7, 5, 7, 8, 6), *K2tog, YO, K2; rep from * 5 (6, 7, 8, 9, 11) more times, K to end. 33 (37, 41, 47, 51, 55) sts.
Row 5: BO 2 sts, K3 (4, 2, 4, 5, 3), *K2tog, YO, K2; rep from * 5 (6, 8, 9, 9, 11) more times, K to end. 31 (35, 39, 45, 49, 53) sts.
Row 7: BO 2 sts, K0 (1, 3, 1, 2, 0), *K2tog, YO, K2; rep from * 6 (6, 7, 9, 10, 11) more times, K to end. 29 (33, 37, 43 ,47, 51) sts.
Row 9: BO 1 st, K2 (3, 1, 3, 0, 2), *K2tog, YO, K2; rep from * 5 (6, 7, 8, 10, 10) more times, K to end. 28 (32, 36, 42, 46, 50) sts.
Row 11: BO 1 st, K0 (1, 3, 1, 2, 0), *K2tog, YO, K2; rep from * 5 (6, 6, 7, 9, 11) more times, K to end. 27 (31, 35, 41, 45, 49) sts.
Row 13: BO 1 st, K2 (3, 1, 3, 0, 2), *K2tog, YO, K2; rep from * 4 (5, 7, 8, 9, 10) more times, K to end. 26 (30, 34, 40, 44, 48) sts.
Row 15: K1 (2, 0, 2, 3, 1), *K2tog, YO, K2; rep from * 5 (5, 7, 8, 9, 10) more times, K to end.
Row 17: K0 (1, 3, 1, 2, 0), *K2tog, YO, K2; rep from * 5 (6, 6, 8, 9, 10) more times, K to end.

Finishing
Using Kitchener Stitch, graft Front Right Side to Back Right Side, and Front Left Side to Back Left Side.

Neckband
Using smaller needles, starting at Left Front Shoulder, PU and K 4 sts from straight edge of neck, PU and K 11 sts from curve, K17 held sts, PU and K 11 sts from curve, PU and K 3 sts from Right Front straight edge, PU and K 2 sts from Right Back straight edge, PU and K 4 sts from Right Back curve, K31 Back Neck held sts, PU and K 4 sts from Left Back curve, PU and K 1 st from Left Back straight edge. 88 sts.
Join in the rnd, PM, and work Rev St st for four rnds.
BO all sts.

Weave in ends and block to diagram, making sure to shape the lace sun motif, pulling it taut when blocking.

LEGEND

K
RS: Knit stitch
WS: Purl stitch

Sl
RS: Slip stitch purl-wise, with yarn in back
WS: Slip stitch purl-wise, with yarn in front

YO
Yarn over

K2tog
Knit 2 stitches together as one stitch

SSK
Slip, slip, knit slipped stitches together

M1R
Make 1 right-leaning stitch

M1L
Make 1 left-leaning stitch

K3tog
Knit 3 stitches together as one stitch

SSSK
(Slip 1 knit-wise) three times; insert left-hand needle from the front to the back of all stitches at the same time and knit them together

CDD
Slip first and second stitches together as if to K2tog; knit 1 stitch; pass 2 slipped stitches over the knit stitch

K5tog
Knit 5 stitches together as one stitch

Pattern Repeat
See notes accompanying each chart

Knit:
K69 (77, 85, 97, 105, 113) sts, lowering the number by 4 sts every time a new repeat is added

Sun Lace, Sizes 38.25–46.75"

Sun Lace, Sizes 50.75–58.75"

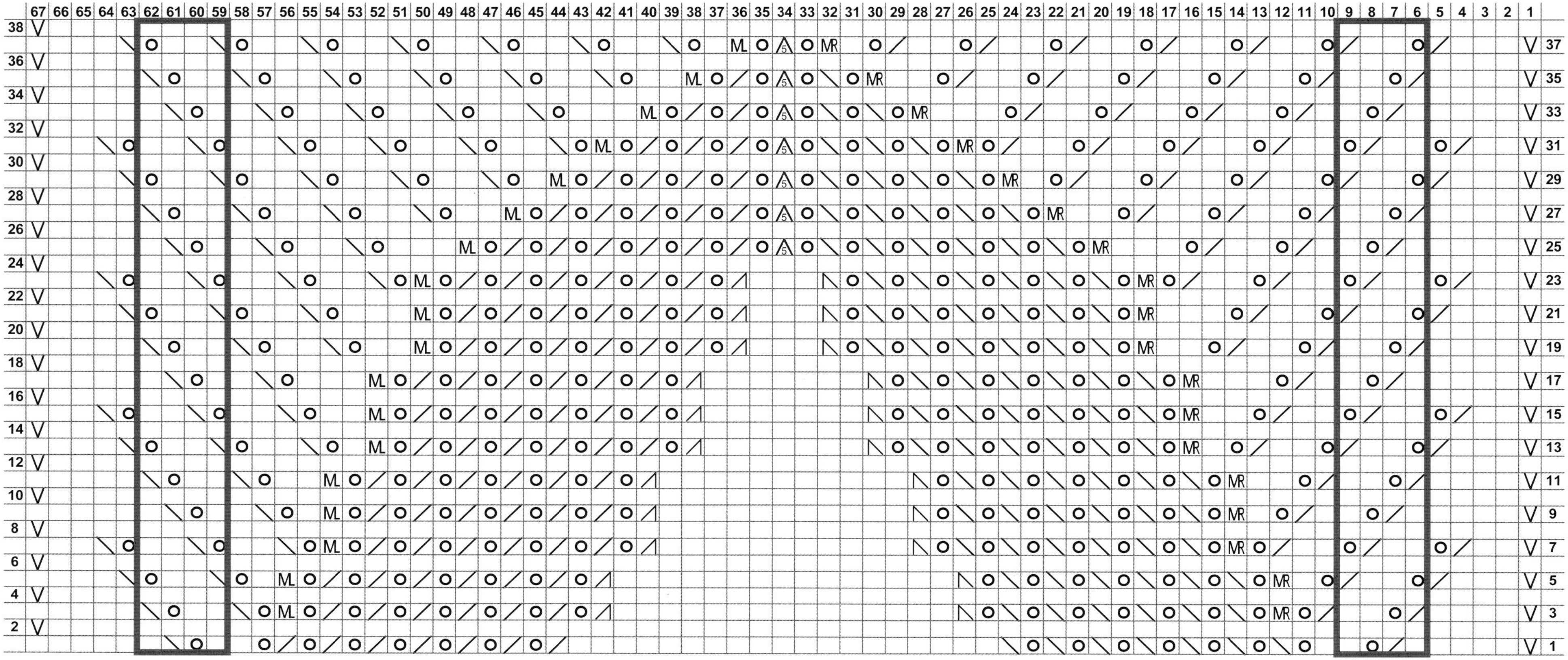

Lace Rays, Sizes 38.25–46.75"

29	28	27	26	25	24	23	22	21	20	19	18	17	16	15	14	13	12	11	10	9	8	7	6	5	4	3	2	1	
8 V								O		\	O		O	/\	O			/			O	\							V 7
6 V			\	O		\	O						O	/\	O				O	\			O	/					V 5
4 V				\	O		\	O					O	/\	O		O	/			O	/							V 3
2 V					\	O		\	O				O	/\	O		O	/		O	/								V 1

Lace Rays, Sizes 50.75–58.75"

35	34	33	32	31	30	29	28	27	26	25	24	23	22	21	20	19	18	17	16	15	14	13	12	11	10	9	8	7	6	5	4	3	2	1	
8 V					\	O		\	O		\	O			O	/\	O		O	/			O	/		O	/						V 7

Front Rays Lace

19	18	17	16	15	14	13	12	11	10	9	8	7	6	5	4	3	2	1	
8 V					O	/				\	O							V 7
6 V				O	/					\	O							V 5
4 V			O	/						\	O						V 3
2 V			O	/						\	O						V 1

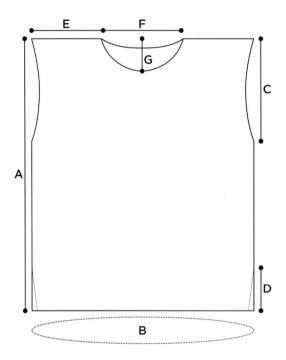

A 25.5 (25.25, 25.5, 26, 26, 26.5)"
B 38.25 (42.75, 46.75, 50.75, 54.75, 58.75)"
C 9.25 (9.5, 10.25, 10.75, 11, 11.75)"
D 4"
E 5.75 (6.75, 7.5, 9, 9.75, 10.75)"
F 7.5"
G 3"

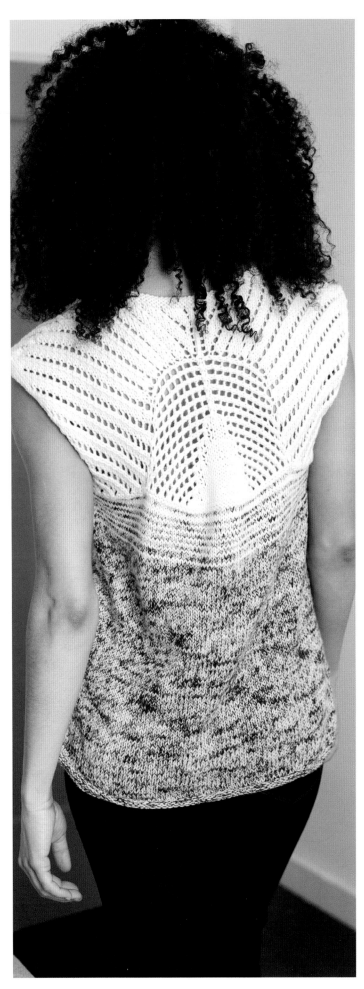
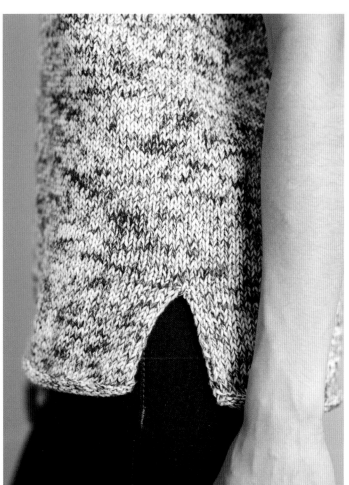

KELDA TEE

by Claire Slade

FINISHED MEASUREMENTS

32 (36, 40, 44, 48, 52, 56, 60, 64)"
finished bust circumference; meant
to be worn with 4–5" positive ease
Sample is 40" size; model is 33.5" bust

YARN

Shine™ (sport weight, 60% Pima Cotton,
40% Modal® natural beech wood fiber;
110 yards/50g): Reef 25335, 6 (7, 7, 8, 9,
11, 13, 14, 15) skeins

NEEDLES

US 5 (3.75 mm) 24–32" circular needles,
and DPNs, or size to obtain gauge

US 5 (3.75mm) extra DPN or straight
or circular needle for 3-Needle Bind Off
US 4 (3.5mm) 16" circular needles, and
DPNs, or one size smaller than size used
to obtain gauge

NOTIONS

Yarn Needle
Two Stitch Markers
Scrap Yarn or Stitch Holders

GAUGE

20 sts and 24 rnds = 4" in Stockinette
Stitch in the round, blocked
18 sts and 22 rnds = 4" in Lace Pattern
in the round, blocked

For pattern support, contact verilyknits@gmail.com

Kelda Tee

Notes:

Kelda is a light and airy top with an interesting lower openwork border, designed to be worn with positive ease. With its slightly cropped length, this top works well as part of a casual or more formal outfit.

Kelda is knit in the round from the bottom up with armhole gussets incorporated for better fitting sleeves. From the armhole divide, the front and back are each worked flat, shoulders are joined, and stitches picked up for the short sleeves and neckline.

Chart is worked in the round; read each chart row from right to left as a RS row.

Lace Pattern (in the round over a multiple of 10 sts)
Rnd 1: P1, YO, SSK, K5, K2tog, YO.
Rnd 2 (and all even-number rnds): P1, K9.
Rnd 3: P1, K1, YO, SSK, K3, K2tog, YO, K1.
Rnd 5: P1, K2, YO, SSK, K1, K2tog, YO, K2.
Rnd 7: P1, K3, YO, SK2P, YO, K3.
Rnd 9: P1, SSK, K2, YO, K1, YO, K2, K2tog.
Rnd 11: Rep Rnd 9.
Rnd 13: Rep Rnd 9.
Rnd 14: P1, K9.
Rep Rnds 1-14 for pattern.

DIRECTIONS

Body
Using larger needles, CO 160 (180, 200, 220, 240, 260, 280, 300, 320) sts and join to work in the rnd, being careful not to twist sts; PM for BOR.
Rnd 1: K all.
Rnd 2: P all.
Rnds 3-4: Rep Rnds 1-2.
Rnd 5: K all.
Work Rnds 1-14 of Lace Pattern (from chart or written directions) three times, then Rnds 1-7 once.
Work St st until piece measures 13 (13, 13, 13.5, 14, 14.5, 14.5, 15, 15)" from CO edge.

Armhole Gussets
Rnd 1: K80 (90, 100, 110, 120, 130, 140, 150, 160), PM, K to end.
Rnd 2: (K1, M1L, K to 1 st before M, M1R, K1, SM) two times. 164 (184, 204, 224, 244, 264, 284, 304, 324) sts.
Rnds 3-4: K all.
Row 5: (K2, M1L, K to 2 sts before M, M1R, K2, SM) two times. 168 (188, 208, 228, 248, 268, 288, 308, 328) sts.
Rnds 6-7: K all.

Sizes - (-, -, -, -, 52, 56, 60, 64)" Only
Rnd 8: (K3, M1L, K to 3 sts before M, M1R, K3, SM) two times. - (-, -, -, -, 272, 292, 312, 332) sts.
Rnds 9-10: K all.

Resume All Sizes
Next Rnd: K3 (3, 3, 3, 3, 4, 4, 4, 4) and place on st holder or scrap yarn tog with last 3 (3, 3, 3, 3, 4, 4, 4, 4) sts of previous rnd for underarm, K78 (88, 98, 108, 118, 128, 138, 148, 158) and place on separate holder for Front, K6 (6, 6, 6, 6, 8, 8, 8, 8) and place on separate holder for other underarm, K to end. 78 (88, 98, 108, 118, 128, 138, 148, 158) sts.

Back (worked flat)
Starting with a WS row, work St st until piece measures 6.25 (6.5, 6.75, 7, 8, 8.5, 9.5, 10, 10.5)" from beginning of armhole, ending on a WS row.

Shape Shoulders
Short Row 1 (RS): K to last 6 (7, 9, 10, 12, 12, 13, 14, 15) sts, W&T.
Short Row 2 (WS): P to last 6 (7, 9, 10, 12, 12, 13, 14, 15) sts, W&T.
Short Row 3: K to last 11 (13, 17, 19, 23, 23, 25, 27, 29) sts, W&T.
Short Row 4: P to last 11 (13, 17, 19, 23, 23, 25, 27, 29) sts, W&T.
Short Row 5: K5 (7, 7, 9, 9, 12, 13, 16, 19), turn (no wrap).
Short Row 6: P to end, picking up wraps.
Break yarn and place the first 16 (20, 24, 28, 32, 35, 38, 43, 48) sts on holder for right shoulder, place next 46 (48, 50, 52, 54, 58, 62, 62, 62) sts on separate holder for back neck. Rejoin yarn and K to end, picking up wraps. Break yarn and place these 16 (20, 24, 28, 32, 35, 38, 43, 48) sts on holder for left shoulder.

Front (worked flat)
With WS facing, return held 78 (88, 98, 108, 118, 128, 138, 148, 158) sts to needle and rejoin yarn.
Work St st until piece measures 4.25 (4.5, 4.75, 5, 6, 6.5, 7.5, 8, 8.5)", ending on a RS row.
Next Row (WS): P22 (26, 30, 34, 38, 41, 44, 49, 54) and place on holder for right front, P34 (36, 38, 40, 42, 46, 50, 50, 50) and place on separate holder for front neck, P to end. 22 (26, 30, 34, 38, 41, 44, 49, 54) sts.

Left Front
Row 1 (RS): K to last 2 sts, K2tog. 1 st dec.
Row 2 (WS): P across.
Rep Rows 1-2 four more times, then rep Row 1 once more. 16 (20, 24, 28, 32, 35, 38, 43, 48) sts.

Shape Shoulder
Short Row 1 (WS): P to last 6 (7, 9, 10, 12, 12, 13, 14, 15) sts, W&T.
Short Row 2 and all RS rows: K to end.
Short Row 3: P to last 11 (13, 17, 19, 23, 23, 25, 27, 29) sts, W&T.
Short Row 5: P to end, picking up all wraps.
Break yarn and place sts on holder.

Right Front
With RS facing, return held 22 (26, 30, 34, 38, 41, 44, 49, 54) sts to needle and rejoin yarn.
Row 1 (RS): SSK, K to end. 1 st dec.
Row 2 (WS): P across.
Rep Rows 1-2 five more times. 16 (20, 24, 28, 32, 35, 38, 43, 48) sts.

Shape Shoulder

Short Row 1 (RS): K to last 6 (7, 9, 10, 12, 12, 13, 14, 15) sts, W&T.

Short Row 2 and all WS rows: P to end.

Short Row 3: K to last 11 (13, 17, 19, 23, 23, 25, 27, 29) sts, W&T.

Short Row 5: K to end, picking up all wraps.

Return right back shoulder sts to separate needle; with WSs facing outwards, join right front shoulder sts to right back shoulder sts using 3-Needle Bind Off.
Rep for left shoulder sts.

Sleeves (make two the same)

With RS facing, rejoin yarn to lower edge of armhole and, using larger needles, PU and K 26 (28, 30, 32, 36, 40, 44, 46, 48) sts up one side, then PU and K 26 (28, 30, 32, 36, 40, 44, 46, 48) sts down the other side, K across held 6 (6, 6, 6, 6, 8, 8, 8, 8) sts, PM for BOR, join to work in the rnd. 58 (62, 66, 70, 78, 88, 96, 100, 104) sts.

Work St st until sleeve measures 2.25 (2, 1.75, 1.5, 1.5, 1.5, 1.5, 1.5, 1.5)".

Change to smaller needles.

Edging

Rnd 1: P all.

Rnd 2: K all.

Rnds 3–4: Rep Rnds 1–2.

BO all sts loosely.

Neckline

With RS facing, rejoin yarn to top left shoulder and, using smaller needles, PU and K 12 sts down left front, K34 (36, 38, 40, 42, 46, 50, 50, 50) held front neck sts, PU and K 12 sts up right front, PU and K 1 st down right back, K46 (48, 50, 52, 54, 58, 62, 62, 62) held back neck sts, PU and K 1 st up left back, join to work in the rnd. 106 (110, 114, 118, 122, 130, 138, 138, 138) sts.

Rnd 1: P all.

Rnd 2: K all.

Rnds 3–4: Rep Rnds 1–2.

BO all sts loosely.

Finishing

Weave in ends, wash, and block to diagram.

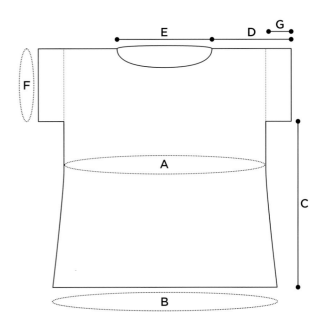

A   32 (36, 40, 44, 48, 52, 56, 60, 64)"

B   35.5 (40, 44.5, 49, 53.25, 57.75, 62.25, 66.5, 71)"

C   14.25 (14.25, 14.25, 14.75, 15.25, 16.25, 16.25, 16.75, 16.75)"

D   6.5 (7, 7.5, 8, 9, 9.5, 10, 11, 12)"

E   8.25 (8.5, 9, 9.5, 9.75, 10.5, 11.5, 11.5, 11.5)"

F   11.5 (12.5, 13.25, 14, 15.5, 17.5, 19.25, 20, 20.75)"

G   2.25 (2, 1.75, 1.5, 1.5, 1.5, 1.5, 1.5, 1.5)"

Lace Pattern

10	9	8	7	6	5	4	3	2	1		
									●	14
/			O		O				●	13
									●	12
/			O		O				●	11
									●	10
/			O		O				●	9
									●	8
			O	⋀	O				●	7
									●	6
		O	/			\	O		●	5
									●	4
	O	/					\	O	●	3
									●	2
O	/						\	O	●	1

LEGEND

☐ **Knit Stitch**

● **Purl Stitch**

O **YO**
Yarn over

/ **K2tog**
Knit 2 stitches together as one stitch

\ **SSK**
Slip, slip, knit slipped stitches together

⋀ **SK2P**
Slip 1 knit-wise, K2tog, pass slip stitch over K2tog

ORCHID BLOSSOM STOLE

by Irina Lyubaeva

FINISHED MEASUREMENTS
71.5″ x 20.5″

YARN
Comfy™ (fingering weight, 75% Pima Cotton, 25% Acrylic; 218 yards/50g): Peony 24818, 6 skeins

NEEDLES
US 4 (3.5mm) straight or circular needles (16″ or longer), or size to obtain gauge

NOTIONS
Yarn Needle
Stitch Markers
Blocking Pins

GAUGE
24 sts and 31 rows = 4″ in Orchid Blossom Lace pattern, blocked

For pattern support, contact anion.khv@gmail.com

Orchid Blossom Stole

Notes:

This stole reflects the beauty of gorgeous blooming orchids. The Orchid Blossom Stole is an elegant lace rectangular shawl featuring a beautiful lace pattern that is very easy to memorize.

It begins with a Garter Stitch border at the bottom, and it is worked flat in one piece. The Garter edging on the sides is worked simultaneously with the body.

Instructions are both written and charted. Chart is worked flat; only RS rows (odd numbers) are shown on chart—read all RS chart rows from right to left. All WS rows are worked: K6, P to last 6 sts, K6.

Orchid Blossom Lace (flat over a multiple of 16 sts plus 12)

Row 1 (RS): K6, (K5, YO, SKP, K2, K2tog, YO, K5) to last 6 sts, K6.

Row 2 and all WS rows through Row 36: K6, P to last 6 sts, K6.

Row 3: K6, *K3, (K2tog, YO, K1, YO, SKP) two times, K3; rep from * to last 6 sts, K6.

Row 5: K6, *K2, (K2tog, YO, K2, YO, SKP) two times, K2; rep from * to last 6 sts, K6.

Row 7: K6, *K1, (K2tog, YO, K3, YO, SKP) two times, K1; rep from * to last 6 sts, K6.

Row 9: K6, (K2tog, YO, K4, YO, SKP) to last 6 sts, K6.

Row 11: Rep Row 9.

Row 13: K6, *(K2tog, YO, K2) two times, (K2, YO, SKP) two times; rep from * to last 6 sts, K6.

Row 15: K6, *(K2tog, YO, K1) two times, K4, (K1, YO, SKP) two times; rep from * to last 6 sts, K6.

Row 17: K6, *(K2tog, YO) two times, K8, (YO, SKP) two times; rep from * to last 6 sts, K6.

Row 19: K6, (K1, K2tog, YO, K10, YO, SKP, K1) to last 6 sts, K6.

Row 21: K6, (K2tog, YO, K1, YO, SKP, K6, K2tog, YO, K1, YO, SKP) to last 6 sts, K6.

Row 23: K6, (K2tog, YO, K2, YO, SKP, K4, K2tog, YO, K2, YO, SKP) to last 6 sts, K6.

Row 25: K6, (K2tog, YO, K3, YO, SKP, K2, K2tog, YO, K3, YO, SKP) to last 6 sts, K6.

Row 27: K6, (K2tog, YO, K4, YO, SKP) to last 6 sts, K6.

Row 29: Rep Row 27.

Row 31: K6, *(K2, YO, SKP) two times, (K2tog, YO, K2) two times; rep from * to last 6 sts, K6.

Row 33: K6, (K3, YO, SKP, K1, YO, SKP, K2tog, YO, K1, K2tog, YO, K3) to last 6 sts, K6.

Row 35: K6, *K4, (YO, SKP) two times, (K2tog, YO) two times, K4; rep from * to last 6 sts, K6.

Rep Rows 1–36 for pattern.

DIRECTIONS

Border
Loosely CO 124 sts.
Knit seven rows.

Body
Work Rows 1–36 of Orchid Blossom Lace pattern 15 times or until desired length is reached, ending with a WS row.

Border
Knit seven rows.
Loosely BO all sts.

Finishing
Weave in ends.
Place shawl in lukewarm water until it is soaking wet (10–15 minutes). Carefully squeeze the water out of the shawl, being careful not to twist the fabric, then roll shawl in a towel and squeeze to remove more water. The shawl should only be moist. Carefully stretch shawl out to size and fasten with pins. Let dry completely, then unpin.

Orchid Blossom Lace

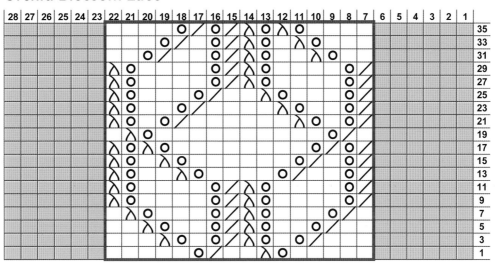

| 28 | 27 | 26 | 25 | 24 | 23 | 22 | 21 | 20 | 19 | 18 | 17 | 16 | 15 | 14 | 13 | 12 | 11 | 10 | 9 | 8 | 7 | 6 | 5 | 4 | 3 | 2 | 1 | |

Row numbers (right side, bottom to top): 1, 3, 5, 7, 9, 11, 13, 15, 17, 19, 21, 23, 25, 27, 29, 31, 33, 35

LEGEND

☐ **Knit Stitch**

⊙ **YO**
Yarn over

⧄ **K2tog**
Knit 2 stitches together as one stitch

⋏ **SKP**
Slip 1 knit-wise, knit 1, pass slip stitch over knit stitch

☐ **Pattern Repeat**

▨ **Yellow = Garter Stitch**
Knit both right side and following wrong side

☐ **White = Stockinette Stitch**
Purl the following wrong side stitch

PEEKABACK TANK

by Adrienne Larsen

FINISHED MEASUREMENTS

34 (38.25, 41.75, 46, 59.75, 54.25, 58, 62)"
finished bust circumference; meant to be
worn with 2–4" positive ease
Sample is 38.25" size; model is 33.5" bust

YARN

Lindy Chain™ (fingering weight, 70%
Linen, 30% Pima Cotton; 180 yards/50g):
MC Mist 27004, 5 (5, 6, 6, 7, 8, 8, 9) balls;
CC Plum 26462, 2 (2, 2, 2, 3, 3, 3, 3) balls

NEEDLES

US 4 (3.5mm) 24–60" circular needles,
or size to obtain gauge
Extra needle, same size

NOTIONS

Yarn Needle
Stitch Markers
Scrap Yarn or Stitch Holder

GAUGE

26 sts and 43 rows = 4" in Stockinette
Stitch, blocked
25 sts and 40 rows = 4" in Lace Pattern,
blocked

For pattern support, contact adrienne.larsen@gmail.com

Peekabank Tank

Notes:

This tank is ready for a day at the beach or a night on the town. The waist shaping is fit to flatter.

The main body of the tank is knit in one piece from the bottom up. The lace panel is knit separately and sewn to the main body.

Chart is worked flat; read RS rows (odd numbers) from right to left, and WS rows (even numbers) from left to right.

RLI (right lifted increase)
With RH needle, K into right shoulder of st in row directly below the next st on LH needle. 1 st inc.

LLI (left lifted increase)
Use LH needle to pick up st 2 rows directly below last st worked and K into it. 1 st inc.

M1R P-wise (make 1 right-leaning stitch, purl-wise)
Inserting LH needle from back to front, PU the horizontal strand between the st just worked and the next st, and P.

M1L P-wise (make 1 left-leaning stitch, purl-wise)
Inserting LH needle from front to back, PU the horizontal strand between the st just worked and the next st, and P TBL.

DIRECTIONS

Body
With MC, CO 32 (38, 41, 44, 48, 51, 58, 60) sts for Back first side, PM, CO 118 (130, 144, 156, 170, 182, 196, 208) sts for Front, PM, CO 32 (38, 41, 44, 48, 51, 58, 60) sts for other Back side. 182 (206, 226, 244, 266, 284, 312, 328) sts.
Dec and Inc rows are worked simultaneously—read through entire section before beginning.
Row 1 and all RS Rows: K across.
Row 2 (WS): K across.
Row 4: K2, P to last 2 sts, K2.
Rep Rows 3–4 19 (19, 13, 10, 10, 10, 11, 11) more times.

Back Inc Row (RS): K2, RLI, work to last 2 sts LLI, K2. 2 sts inc.
Cont as established while working Back Inc Row every 40 (42, 30, 22, 24, 24, 24, 20) rows a total of 3 (2, 2, 7, 2, 6, 7, 8) times, then every 0 (40, 28, 0, 22, 22, 0, 18) rows 0 (1, 3, 0, 5, 1, 0, 1) time(s). 6 (6, 10, 14, 14, 14, 14, 18) sts inc.

AT THE SAME TIME
Starting with first row after CO, work 8 (8, 8, 8, 8, 8, 6, 6) rows as indicated above.
Dec Row (RS): (K to 2 sts before next M, SSK, SM, K2tog) two times, K to end. 2 sts dec Front, 1 st dec each Back side, 116 (128, 142, 154, 168, 180, 194, 206) sts for Front.
Cont as established while working Dec Row every 10 (10, 10, 10, 10, 10, 8, 8) rows a total of 6 (3, 5, 6, 7, 9, 11, 6) times, then every 8 (8, 8, 8, 8, 0, 6, 6) rows 2 (6, 4, 3, 2, 0, 1, 8) time(s). 16 (18, 18, 18, 18, 18, 24, 28) sts dec Front, 8 (9, 9, 9, 9, 9, 12, 14) sts dec each Back side, 100 (110, 124, 136, 150, 162, 170, 178) sts for Front.

Work for 21 rows, cont Back Inc Rows if applicable.

Waist Inc Row (RS): (K to M, RLI, SM, LLI) two times, K to end. 2 sts inc Front, 1 st inc each Back side, 102 (112, 126, 138, 152, 164, 172, 180) sts for Front.
Cont as established until two rows before final Back Inc Row, while working Waist Inc Row every 10 (8, 10, 8, 10, 8, 6, 6) rows a total of 3 (6, 5, 4, 4, 1, 1, 11) time(s), then every 12 (0, 0, 10, 12, 10, 8, 0) rows 1 (0, 0, 2, 1, 5, 7, 0) time(s), ending with a RS Row. 8 (12, 10, 12, 10, 12, 16, 22) sts inc for Front, 4 (6, 5, 6, 5, 6, 8, 11) sts inc for each Back side; 110 (124, 136, 150, 162, 176, 188, 202) Front sts, 31 (38, 42, 48, 51, 55, 61, 66) each Back side sts; 172 (200, 220, 246, 264, 286, 310, 334) sts total.

Next Row (WS): *Work as established to 10 (12, 15, 20, 24, 31, 36, 43) sts before next M, K20 (24, 30, 40, 48, 62, 72, 86); rep from * once more, work to end of row.
Next Row: Work Back Inc Row. 32 (39, 43, 49, 52, 56, 62, 67) Back sts; 174 (202, 222, 248, 266, 288, 312, 336) sts total.

Separate for Underarm
Next Row (WS): *Work as established to 10 (12, 15, 20, 24, 31, 36, 43) sts before next M, P2, BO 16 (20, 26, 36, 44, 58, 68, 82) sts P-wise, P2; rep from * once more, work in pattern to end of row. 94 (104, 110, 114, 118, 118, 120, 120) sts for Front, 24 (29, 30, 31, 30, 27, 28, 26) sts for each Back side.
Place Right Back and Front sts on st holder or scrap yarn.

Left Back
Row 1 (RS): K across.
Row 2 (WS): K2, P to last 2 sts, K2.
Work Rows 1–2 once more.
Inc Row (RS): K2, RLI, K to end. 1 st inc, 25 (30, 31, 32, 31, 28, 29, 27) sts.
Cont as established while working Inc Row every four rows another 15 (17, 18, 20, 19, 19, 22, 22) times, then every two rows 5 (3, 4, 3, 7, 10, 7, 9) times. 20 (20, 22, 23, 26, 29, 29, 31) sts inc, 45 (50, 53, 55, 57, 57, 58, 58) sts.
Next Row (WS): Work to last 2 sts, M1R P-wise, K2. 1 st inc.
Next Row (RS): K2, RLI, K to end. 1 st inc.
Rep last two rows once more. 49 (54, 57, 59, 61, 61, 62, 62) sts.
Place sts on st holder or scrap yarn.

Right Back
Place Right Back sts on needles and join yarn to RS.
Row 1 (RS): K across.
Row 2 (WS): K2, P to last 2 sts, K2.
Work Rows 1–2 once more.
Inc Row (RS): K to last 2 sts, LLI, K2. 1 st inc, 25 (30, 31, 32, 31, 28, 29, 27) sts.
Cont as established while working Inc Row every four rows another 15 (17, 18, 20, 19, 19, 22, 22) times, then every two rows 5 (3, 4, 3, 7, 10, 7, 9) times. 20 (20, 22, 23, 26, 29, 29, 31) sts inc, 45 (50, 53, 55, 57, 57, 58, 58) sts.
Next Row (WS): K2, M1L P-wise, work to end of row. 1 st inc.
Next Row (RS): K to last 2 sts, LLI, K2. 1 st inc.

Rep last two rows once more. 49 (54, 57, 59, 61, 61, 62, 62) sts. Place sts on st holder or scrap yarn.

Front

Place 94 (104, 110, 114, 118, 118, 120, 120) Front sts on needles and join yarn to RS of work.
Row 1 (RS): K across.
Row 2 (WS): K2, P to last 2 sts, K2.
Rep Rows 1–2 until piece measures 7 (7.5, 8, 8.5, 8.75, 9. 5, 10, 10.25)" from underarm BO, ending with a WS Row.

Shape Shoulders

Short Rows 1–2: Work as established to last 2 sts, W&T.
Short Rows 3–4: Work as established to last 4 sts, W&T.
Short Rows 5–6: Work as established to last 7 sts, W&T.
Short Rows 7–8: Work as established to last 10 sts, W&T.
Short Rows 9–10: Work as established to last 13 sts, W&T.
Short Row 11 (RS): Work to end of row, hiding wraps.
Row 12 (WS): K2, P to last 2 sts, K2, hiding wraps.
Turn work inside out.
Row 13: With RSs facing each other, attach 13 Front sts to Back sts using 3-Needle Bind Off, K68 (78, 84, 88, 92, 92, 94, 94) Front sts, attach 13 Front sts to Back using 3-Needle BO.

Neckline

Place Front neck sts on needles with RS facing, place Right Back neck sts on same needles, place Left Back neck sts on extra needle with RS facing. Join yarn to RS of Front neck sts.
Note: The two center back sts of the Left Back will overlap those of the Right Back
Rnd 1: Knit to last 2 Right Back sts on needle (at center back), (K1 from Right Back tog with 1 st from Left Back) two times, K to end of Left Back sts, join to work in the rnd and PM for BOR. 138 (158, 170, 178, 186, 186, 190, 190) sts.
Rnd 2: P all.
Rnd 3: K all.
BO P-wise.

Lace Panel

With CC, CO 57 (57, 63, 69, 75, 81, 81, 87) sts.
Row 1 (RS): K across.
Row 2 (WS): K across.
Work Lace Pattern until piece measures 22.25 (23.25, 24.25, 25.25, 26, 27.25, 28.25, 29)", ending with a RS row.
BO P-wise.

Finishing

With RS of Lace Panel facing WS of Body, and Garter edge of Body overlapping panel, whip stitch Lace Panel in place. Note that Body will cover sides of panel on upper portions. Weave in ends, wash, and block to diagram.

Lace Pattern

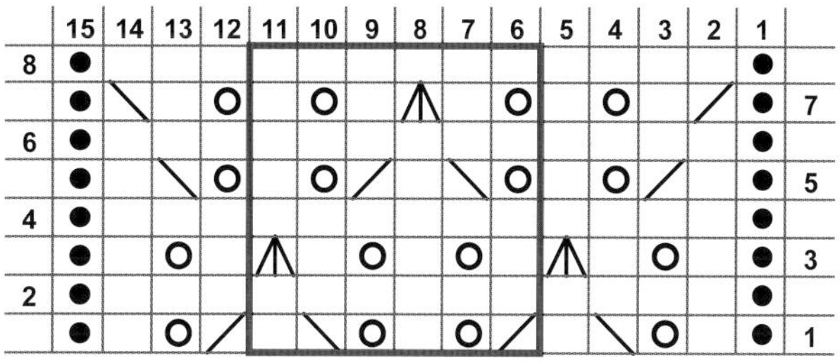

	15	14	13	12	11	10	9	8	7	6	5	4	3	2	1	
8	●														●	
	●	\		O		O		⋀		O		O		/	●	7
6	●														●	
	●		\	O		O	/		\	O		O	/		●	5
4	●														●	
	●		O		⋀		O		O		⋀		O		●	3
2	●														●	
	●		O	/		\	O		O	/		\	O		●	1

LEGEND

K
RS: Knit stitch
WS: Purl stitch

P
RS: Purl stitch
WS: Knit stitch

YO
Yarn over

K2tog
Knit 2 stitches together as one stitch

SSK
Slip, slip, knit slipped stitches together

CDD
Slip first and second stitches together as if to K2tog; knit 1 stitch; pass 2 slipped stitches over the knit stitch

Pattern Repeat

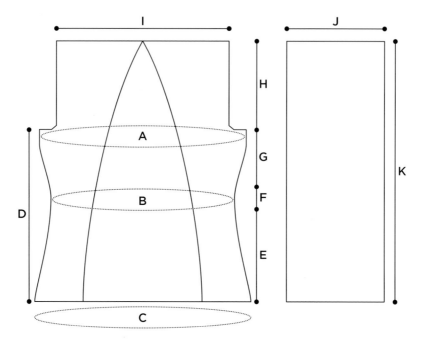

A 34 (38.25, 41.75, 46, 59.75, 54.25, 58, 62)"
B 30.75 (34, 38, 41.75, 46.25, 50, 52.5, 54.5)"
C 36.5 (40, 44.25, 48, 52.25, 56, 60.5, 63.75)"
D 15 (15.5, 16.25, 16.5, 17, 17.75, 18, 18.5)"
E 8 (8.25, 8.5, 8.75, 9, 9.25, 9.5, 9.75)"
F 2"
G 5 (5.25, 5.5, 5.75, 6, 6.25, 6.5, 6.75)"
H 7.25 (7.75, 8.25, 8.75, 9, 9.75, 10.25, 10.5)"
I 14.5 (16, 17, 17.5, 18.25, 18.25, 18.5, 18.5)"

J 9 (9, 10, 11, 12, 13, 13, 14)"
K 22.25 (23.25, 24.25, 25.25, 26, 27.25, 28.25, 29)"

SUNLIGHT THROUGH ASPENS WRAP

by Kalurah Hudson

FINISHED MEASUREMENTS
18 (20, 23.5)" x 50 (60, 70)"
Sample is 20x60" size; model is 33.5" bust

YARN
CotLin™ (DK weight, 70% Tanguis Cotton, 30% Linen; 123 yards/50g): Sagebrush 25777, 5 (5, 9) skeins

NEEDLES
US 6 (4mm) 32" or longer circular needles, or size to obtain gauge

NOTIONS
Yarn Needle
Locking Stitch Marker
Blocking Pins
0.5" Button(s) (you choose how many) and Matching Thread

GAUGE
17 sts and 21 rows = 4" worked over first 17 stitches of Sunlight Through Aspens Pattern, blocked

For pattern support, contact kalurah@whiletheyplay.com

Sunlight Through Aspens Wrap

Notes:

This versatile wrap is knit in a light and airy ribbed lace stitch. The easy-to-memorize stitch is also reversible, and the pretty eyelet lace edging is knit at the same time as the rest of the wrap, making it totally seamless.

Wear the wrap asymmetrically, over one shoulder, or with the buttoned section down the center, as a poncho. The pattern is written for three sizes.

The wrap can be worked from written instructions or from the chart. Chart is worked flat; read RS rows (odd numbers) from right to left, and WS rows (even numbers) from left to right. Repeat pattern repeat stitches (in red box) the appropriate number of times to complete the chart row.

Don't forget to swatch. Gauge is critical for this pattern. The total number of skeins of yarn for each size allows enough yardage to make a gauge swatch.

Sunlight Through Aspens Pattern (worked flat)

Row 1 (RS): K3, (P1, K2tog, YO, P1, K3) 7 (8, 10) times, P1, K2, YO, SSK, P1, K1, (YO twice, K2tog) two times, K1. 66, (73, 87) sts.

Row 2 (WS): K3, (P1, K2) two times, P2, YO, P2tog, (K1, P3, K1, P2) 7 (8, 10) times, K4.

Row 3: K3, (P1, YO, SSK, P1, K3) 7 (8, 10) times, P1, K2, YO, SSK, P1, K3, (YO twice, K2tog) two times, K1. 68, (75, 89) sts.

Row 4: K3, P1, K2, P1, K4, P2, YO, P2tog, (K1, P3, K1, P2) 7 (8, 10) times, K4.

Row 5: K3, (P1, K2tog, YO, P1, K3) 7 (8, 10) times, P1, K2, YO, SSK, P1, K5, (YO twice, K2tog) two times, K1. 70, (77, 91) sts.

Row 6: K3, P1, K2, P1, K6, P2, YO, P2tog, (K1, P3, K1, P2) 7 (8, 10) times, K4.

Row 7: K3, (P1, YO, SSK, P1, K3) 7 (8, 10) times, P1, K2, YO, SSK, P1, K7, (YO twice, K2tog) two times, K1. 72, (79, 93) sts.

Row 8: K3, P1, K2, P1, K8, P2, YO, P2tog, (K1, P3, K1, P2) 7 (8, 10) times, K4.

Row 9: K3, (P1, K2tog, YO, P1, K3) 7 (8, 10) times, P1, K2, YO, SSK, P1, K9, (YO twice, K2tog) two times, K1. 74, (81, 95) sts.

Row 10: K3, P1, K2, P1, K10, P2, YO, P2tog, (K1, P3, K1, P2) 7 (8, 10) times, K4.

Row 11: K3, (P1, YO, SSK, P1, K3) 7 (8, 10) times, P1, K2, YO, SSK, P1, K16.

Row 12: BO 10 sts (1 st remains on needle from completing BO), K6, P2, YO, P2tog, (K1, P3, K1, P2) 7 (8, 10) times, K4. 64, (71, 85) sts.

Rep Rows 1–12 for pattern.

DIRECTIONS

Loosely CO 64 (71, 85) sts.

Using either Sunlight Through Aspens Pattern chart or written instructions, work Rows 1–12 a total of 20 (24, 28) times, stopping after Row 11 of final rep.

Bind Off Row (WS): On Row 12 of final pattern rep, BO all live sts across entire row K-wise. Break yarn and pull through remaining st.

Finishing

Weave in all ends, wash, and block.

Assemble wrap by folding it together lengthwise with WS facing each other. Measure 18 (20, 22)" in from fold and mark this point with a locking st marker or safety pin. Attach buttons with matching thread to the WS of one side of the wrap, lining up each button with an eyelet from RS of wrap. Attach as many buttons as you like.

Alternatively, fold the wrap tog with RS facing each other and seam wrap using a whip stitch. Turn wrap RS out.

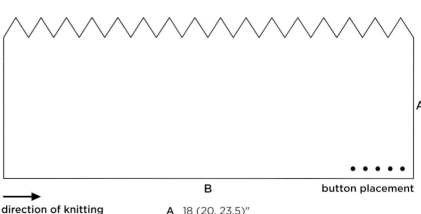

direction of knitting

button placement

A 18 (20, 23.5)"

B 50 (60, 70)"

Sunlight Through Aspens Pattern

Chart columns (right to left): 32 31 30 29 28 27 26 25 24 23 22 21 20 19 18 17 16 15 14 13 12 11 10 9 8 7 6 5 4 3 2 1

Rows: 1–12

LEGEND

No Stitch
Placeholder—no stitch made

K
RS: Knit stitch
WS: Purl stitch

P
RS: Purl stitch
WS: Knit stitch

YO
Yarn over

K2tog
RS: Knit 2 stitches together as one stitch
WS: Purl 2 stitches together as one stitch

SSK
Slip, slip, knit slipped stitches together

BO
Bind off 1 stitch

BO st
Stitch remaining on needle
after working bind off stitches

Pattern Repeat

TALES OF SPRING TANK

by Danae Smith

FINISHED MEASUREMENTS

32.5 (36.75, 40.75, 44.25, 48.5, 52.75)"
finished bust circumference with box
pleats partially open; pleats allow for
up to an extra 1" of fit
Sample is 36.75" size; model is 33.5" bust

YARN

CotLin™ Reflections (DK weight, 70%
Tanguis Cotton, 30% Linen; 246
yards/100g): Nimbus 27870, 3 (3, 4,
4, 5, 5) hanks

NEEDLES

US 7 (4.5mm) 16" circular needles,
and 32" circular needles, or size to
obtain gauge

US 7 (4.5mm) DPNs for pleats (bamboo
or wood needles work best to prevent
stitches from sliding off)

NOTIONS

Yarn Needle
Stitch Markers
Locking Stitch Markers
Scrap Yarn or Stitch Holder
Cable Needle

GAUGE

17 sts and 27 rnds = 4" in Stockinette
Stitch in the round, blocked
24 sts and 27 rows = 4" in Panel Chart
pattern, blocked

For pattern support, contact ottercraftworks@gmail.com

Tales of Spring Tank

Notes:

Tales of Spring was inspired by stories of a magical land where wearing knits is not confined to a few months of false winter. Knitters can show off their skills year-round and even wear a knitted tank to a spring picnic without worrying about being crushed by humidity.

This tank is worked in the round from the bottom up. The scalloped hem is accomplished by working short rows on both the back and front. The box pleat at the straps creates ease when worn, but could be tacked closed if a tighter fit is desired. Note that the strap seam sits forward of the shoulder. Final strap length can be shortened for a snugger fit in the back.

The Panel Chart is worked both in the round and flat in this pattern. When worked in the round, read each chart row from right to left as a RS row. When worked flat, read RS rows (odd numbers) from right to left, and WS rows (even numbers) from left to right.

DIRECTIONS

Ruffle Hem

With 32″ circulars, CO 378 (420, 462, 504, 546, 588) sts. Join in the rnd, being careful not to twist sts. PM for BOR.
Note: If worried about twisting so many sts, wait to join in the rnd until after pleats. Work St st in flat rows, work Ruffle Pleat row flat, then join in the rnd and cont pattern as written. Seam edges of St st section during finishing.

Work St st until piece measures 1″.

Ruffle Pleat Rnd: (K3, work Ruffle Pleat) to end. 216 (240, 264, 288, 312, 336) sts dec; 18 (20, 22, 24, 26, 28) pleats; 162 (180, 198, 216, 234, 252) total sts.

Next Rnd: K73 (83, 89, 99, 109, 113), PM for center of right armscye, K26 (28, 30, 32, 34, 37), PM for Panel Chart, K37 (41, 49, 53, 57, 65), PM, K to end.

Short Rows

Note: Work wraps tog with wrapped sts as encountered.
Short Row 1 (RS): K57 (60, 63, 66, 69, 70), W&T.
Short Row 2 (WS): P39 (37, 35, 33, 31, 27), W&T.
Short Row 3: K to 2 (3, 4, 5, 6, 7) sts past wrapped st, W&T.
Short Row 4: P to 2 (3, 4, 5, 6, 7) sts past wrapped st, W&T.
Rep Short Rows 3–4 four more times.
Short Row 13: K to armscye M, SM, K26 (28, 30, 32, 34, 37), SM, work Row 1 of Panel Chart, SM, K3 (0, 2, 4, 1, 4), W&T.
Short Row 14: P to M, SM, work next row of Panel Chart, SM, P3 (0, 2, 4, 1, 4), W&T.
Short Row 15: K to M, SM, work next row of Panel Chart, SM, K to 3 (4, 4, 4, 5, 5) sts past wrapped st, W&T.
Short Row 16: P to M, SM, work next row of Panel Chart, SM, P to 3 (4, 4, 4, 5, 5) sts past wrapped st, W&T.
Rep Short Rows 15–16 four more times.
Short Row 25: K to M, SM, work next row of Panel Chart, SM, K26 (28, 30, 32, 34, 37).

Ruffle Pleat (worked over 18 sts)
Sl next 6 sts unworked to DPN, Sl 6 more sts unworked to second DPN. Arrange needles so that DPNs form a V pointing toward the front, then fold all three needles on top of each other so that LH circular needle is at the back, the DPN next to it is in the middle and the first DPN is on top. (Insert third DPN through first st on all three needles, knit through all 3 sts like a K3tog dec) six times. 1 pleat worked, 12 sts dec, 6 sts remain.

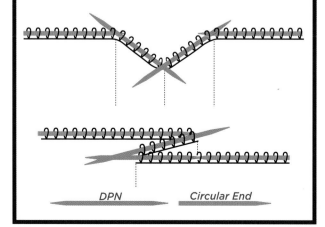

DPN   *Circular End*

Box Pleat
Right Pleat: Sl next 3 (3, 3, 4, 4, 4) sts unworked to DPN, Sl 3 (3, 3, 4, 4, 4) more sts unworked to second DPN. Arrange needles so that DPNs form a V pointing toward the front, then fold all three needles on top of each other so that LH circular needle is at the back, the DPN next to it is in the middle and the first DPN is on top. (Insert third DPN through first st on all three needles, knit through all 3 sts like a K3tog dec) 3 (3, 3, 4, 4, 4) times. Right Pleat worked; 6 (6, 6, 8, 8, 8) sts dec, 3 (3, 3, 4, 4, 4) sts remain.

Left Pleat: Sl next 3 (3, 3, 4, 4, 4) sts unworked to DPN, Sl 3 (3, 3, 4, 4, 4) more sts unworked to second DPN. Arrange needles so that DPNs form a V pointing toward the back, then fold all three needles on top of each other so that first DPN is at the back, the second DPN is in the middle and LH circular is on top. (Insert third DPN through first st on all three needles, knit through all 3 sts like a K3tog dec) 3 (3, 3, 4, 4, 4) times. Left Pleat worked; 6 (6, 6, 8, 8, 8) sts dec, 3 (3, 3, 4, 4, 4) sts remain.

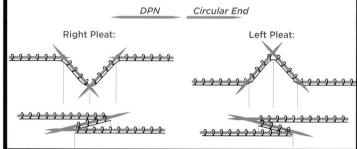

DPN   *Circular End*

Right Pleat: Left Pleat:

Torso

Place locking st M.

Rnd 1: WE as established to end of rnd.

Rep Rnd 1 until piece measures 6 (6, 6.25, 6.25, 6.25, 6.25)" from locking M.

Dec Rnd: K1, SSK, K to 3 sts before M, K2tog, K1, SM, K1, SSK, K to M, SM, work next row of Panel Chart, SM, K to 3 sts before M, K2tog, K1. 4 sts dec, 158 (176, 194, 212, 230, 248) sts.

Cont to rep Rnd 1 until piece measures 10.5 (10.5, 11, 11, 11.25, 11.25)" from locking M.

Rep Dec Rnd. 154 (172, 190, 208, 226, 244) sts.

Cont to rep Rnd 1 until piece measures 18 (18, 18.5, 18.5, 19, 19)" from longest part of CO.

Rep Dec Rnd. 150 (168, 186, 204, 222, 240) sts.

Divide for Front & Back

Setup Rnd: K to 2 (2, 3, 3, 3, 3) sts before M, BO 2 (2, 3, 3, 3, 3) sts, remove M, BO 21 (23, 26, 28, 30, 32) sts, P to 21 (23, 26, 28, 30, 32) before BOR, BO 21 (23, 26, 28, 30, 32) sts, remove BOR M. Place Back sts on st holder or scrap yarn and transfer Front sts to 16" circular needles. 39 (45, 49, 55, 61, 69) Back sts, 67 (75, 82, 90, 98, 104) Front sts.

Front

Setup Row (RS): BO 2 (2, 3, 3, 3, 3) sts, SSK twice, K to last 4 sts, K2tog twice. 61 (69, 75, 83, 91, 97) Front sts.

Row 1 (WS): P across.

Row 2 (RS): SSK 1 (1, 1, 1, 2, 2) time(s), K to last 2 (2, 2, 2, 4, 4) sts, K2tog 1 (1, 1, 1, 2, 2) time(s). 59 (67, 73, 81, 87, 93) sts.

Row 3: P across.

Row 4: SSK, K to last 2 sts, K2tog. 57 (65, 71, 79, 85, 91) sts.

Row 5: P across.

Sizes - (-, -, -, 48.5, 52.75)" Only

Rep Rows 4–5 once more. - (-, -, -, 83, 89) sts.

Resume All Sizes

Row 6: K across.

Row 7: P across.

Rep Rows 6–7 until Front measures 3.5 (3.75, 4, 4, 4.25, 4.5)" from divide, ending with a WS row.

Right Strap Front

Row 1 (RS): K24 (27, 28, 31, 32, 34), BO 9 (11, 15, 17, 19, 21) sts, K24 (27, 28, 31, 32, 34).

Row 2 (WS): P24 (27, 28, 31, 32, 34) sts. Place remaining 24 (27, 28, 31, 32, 34) Left Strap Front sts on st holder.

Row 3: SSK 1 (2, 2, 2, 2, 2) times(s), K22 (23, 24, 27, 28, 30). 23 (25, 26, 29, 30, 32) sts.

Row 4: P across.

Row 5: SSK, K to end. 22 (24, 25, 28, 29, 31) sts.

Row 6: P across.

Sizes - (-, 40.75, -, 48.5, 52.75)" Only

Next Row: SSK, K to end. - (-, 24, -, 28, 30) sts.

Next Row: P across.

Resume All Sizes

Row 7: K across.

Row 8: P across.

Rep Rows 7–8 until strap measures 5.5 (6, 6, 6.5, 6.5, 7)" from divide, ending with a WS row.

Next Row: K2 (3, 3, 2, 2, 3), work Box Pleat (Right Pleat then Left Pleat), K2 (3, 3, 2, 2, 3). 10 (12, 12, 12, 12, 14) sts.

BO P-wise.

Left Strap Front

Return 24 (27, 28, 31, 32, 34) Left Strap Front sts to 16" circular needles. With WS facing, join yarn.

Row 1 (WS): P across.

Row 2 (RS): K to last 2 (4, 4, 4, 4, 4) sts, K2tog 1 (2, 2, 2, 2, 2) time(s). 23 (25, 26, 29, 30, 32) sts.

Row 3: P across.

Row 4: K to last 2 sts, K2tog. 22 (24, 25, 28, 29, 31) sts.

Row 5: P across.

Sizes - (-, 40.75, -, 48.5, 52.75)" Only

Next Row: K to last 2 sts, K2tog. - (-, 24, -, 28, 30) sts.

Next Row: P across.

Resume All Sizes

Work to end of section as for Right Strap Front, beginning with Row 7 (there is no Row 6 for this section).

Racerback

Return 39 (45, 49, 55, 61, 69) Back sts to 16" circular needles. With RS facing, join yarn.

Row 1 (RS): SSK twice, P to last 4 sts, K2tog twice. 4 sts dec.

Row 2 (WS): P2, K to last 2 sts, P2.

Rep Rows 1–2 5 (5, 6, 6, 8, 9) more times. 15 (21, 21, 27, 25, 29) sts.

Size 44.25" Only: SSK, K1, P to last 3 sts, K1, K2tog. 25 sts.

Row 3: K2, P to last 2 sts, K2.

Row 4: P2, K to last 2 sts, P2.

Rep Rows 3–4 until racerback strap measures 5.5 (5.75, 6, 6, 6.25, 6.5)" from divide, ending with a WS row.

Shape Straps

Sizes 32.5 (36.75, -, -, -, -)" Only

Setup Row 1 (RS): K1, M1, P5 (8, -, -, -, -), M1, K3, M1, P5 (8, -, -, -, -), M1, K1. 19 (25, -, -, -, -) sts.

Setup Row 2 (WS): P1, K7 (10, -, -, -, -), P3, K7 (10, -, -, -, -), P1.

Sizes 32.5 (-, 40.75, -, -, -)" Only

Setup Row (RS): K1, M1, P7 (-, 9, -, -, -), K1, Sl1, K1, PSSO, P7 (-, 9, -, -, -), M1, K1. 20 (-, 24, -, -, -) sts.

Sizes - (36.75, -, 44.25, 48.5, 52.75)" Only

Setup Row (RS): K1, P- (10, -, 10, 10, 12), K1, Sl1, K1, PSSO, P- (10, -, 10, 10, 12), K1. - (24, -, 24, 24, 28) sts.

Resume All Sizes

Next Row (WS): P1, K8 (10, 10, 10, 10, 12), P1. Place remaining sts on st holder or scrap yarn. 10 (12, 12, 12, 12, 14) sts per strap.

Left Strap

Row 1 (RS): SSK, P to last st, M1, K1.

Row 2 (WS): P1, K to last st, P1.

Rep Rows 1–2 until Left Strap measures 7.5 (8.25, 9.25, 10.5, 11.25, 12.25)" from Racerback strap split.

BO all sts.

Right Strap

Return remaining strap sts to 16″ circular needle.

With RS facing, join yarn.

Row 1 (RS): K1, M1, P to last 2 sts, K2tog.

Row 2 (WS): P1, K to last st, P1.

Rep Rows 1–2 until Right Strap measures 7.5 (8.25, 9.25, 10.5, 11.25, 12.25)″ from Racerback strap split.

BO all sts.

Finishing

Sew straps tog.

Weave in ends, wash, and block to diagram.

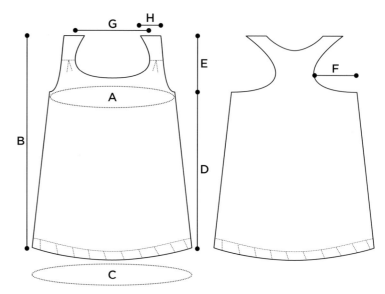

A 29.75 (34, 38, 40.5, 44.75, 49)″

B 24.5 (25, 26, 26.5, 27.5, 28)″

C 38 (42.25, 46.5, 50.75, 55, 59.25)″

D 18 (18, 18.5, 18.5, 19, 19)″

E 6.5 (7, 7.5, 8, 8.5, 9)″

F 5 (5.5, 6, 6.5, 7, 7.5)″

G 8.75 (9.75, 11, 13, 14, 14.25)″

H 2.5 (2.75, 2.75, 2.75, 2.75, 3.25)″

Panel Chart

LEGEND

K
RS: Knit stitch
WS: Purl stitch

P
RS: Purl stitch
WS: Knit stitch

Sl
RS: Slip stitch purl-wise, with yarn in back
WS: Slip stitch purl-wise, with yarn in front

Pattern Repeat
Rep 3 (4, 6, 7, 8, 10) times

Knit Elongated
Knit 1 stitch wrapping yarn twice; drop extra wrap from needle on the next row

Right Twist (RT)
Sl1 to CN, hold in back; K1, K1 from CN

Left Twist (LT)
Sl1 to CN, hold in front; K1, K1 from CN

Glossary
Common Stitches & Techniques

Slipped Stitches (Sl)
Always slip stitches purl-wise with yarn held to the wrong side of work, unless noted otherwise in the pattern.

Make 1 Left-Leaning Stitch (M1L)
Inserting LH needle from front to back, PU the horizontal strand between the st just worked and the next st, and K TBL.

Make 1 Right-Leaning Stitch (M1R)
Inserting LH needle from back to front, PU the horizontal strand between the st just worked and the next st, and K TFL.

Slip, Slip, Knit (SSK)
(Sl1 K-wise) twice; insert LH needle into front of these 2 sts and knit them together.

Centered Double Decrease (CDD)
Slip first and second sts together as if to work K2tog; K1; pass 2 slipped sts over the knit st.

Stockinette Stitch (St st, flat over any number of sts)
Row 1 (RS): Knit all sts.
Row 2 (WS): Purl all sts.
Rep Rows 1-2 for pattern.
St st in the round: Knit every rnd.

Garter Stitch (in the round over any number of sts)
Rnd 1: Purl all sts.
Rnd 2: Knit all sts.
Rep Rnds 1-2 for pattern.
Garter Stitch flat: Knit every row.
(One Garter ridge is comprised of two rows/rnds.)

1x1 Rib (flat or in the round, over an even number of sts)
Row/Rnd 1: (K1, P1) to end of row/rnd.
Rep Row/Rnd 1 for pattern.

2x2 Rib (flat over a multiple of 4 sts plus 2)
Row 1 (RS): K2, (P2, K2) to end of row.
Row 2 (WS): P2, (K2, P2) to end of row.
Rep Rows 1-2 for pattern.

2x2 Rib (in the round over a multiple of 4 sts)
Rnd 1: (K2, P2) to end of rnd.
Rep Rnd 1 for pattern.

Magic Loop Technique
A technique using one long circular needle to knit in the round around a small circumference. A tutorial can be found at tutorials.knitpicks.com/wptutorials/magic-loop.

Knitting in the Round with Two Circular Needles
A technique using two long circulars to knit around a small circumference. A tutorial can be found at tutorials.knitpicks.com/knitting-in-the-round-with-2-circular-needles.

Backward Loop Cast On
A simple, all-purpose cast on that can be worked mid-row. Also called Loop, Single, or E-Wrap Cast On. A tutorial can be found at tutorials.knitpicks.com/loop-cast-on.

Long Tail Cast On
Fast and neat once you get the hang of it. Also referred to as the Slingshot Cast On. A tutorial can be found at tutorials.knitpicks.com/long-tail-cast-on.

Cabled Cast On
A strong and nice looking basic cast on that can be worked mid-project. A tutorial can be found at tutorials.knitpicks.com/cabled-cast-on.

3-Needle Bind Off
Used to easily seam two rows of live stitches together. A tutorial can be found at tutorials.knitpicks.com/3-needle-bind-off.

Abbreviations

approx	approximately	KFB	knit into front and back of stitch	PSSO	pass slipped stitch over	SSP	slip, slip, purl these 2 stitches together through back loop
BO	bind off			PU	pick up		
BOR	beginning of round	K-wise	knit-wise	P-wise	purl-wise	SSSK	slip, slip, slip, knit these 3 stitches together (like SSK)
CN	cable needle	LH	left hand	rep	repeat		
C (1, 2...)	color (1, 2...)	M	marker	Rev St st	reverse stockinette stitch		
CC	contrast color	M1	make 1 stitch			St st	stockinette stitch (*see above*)
CDD	centered double decrease (*see above*)	M1L	make 1 left-leaning stitch (*see above*)	RH	right hand	st(s)	stitch(es)
				rnd(s)	round(s)	TBL	through back loop
CO	cast on	M1R	make 1 right-leaning stitch (*see above*)	RS	right side	TFL	through front loop
cont	continue			Sk	skip	tog	together
dec(s)	decrease(es)	MC	main color	SK2P	slip 1, knit 2 together, pass slipped stitch over	W&T	wrap & turn (for short rows; *see next pg*)
DPN(s)	double pointed needle(s)	P	purl				
		P2tog	purl 2 stitches together	SKP	slip, knit, pass slipped stitch over	WE	work even
inc(s)	increase(s)					WS	wrong side
K	knit	P3tog	purl 3 stitches together	Sl	slip (*see above*)	WYIB	with yarn in back
K2tog	knit 2 stitches together	PM	place marker	SM	slip marker	WYIF	with yarn in front
		PFB	purl into front and back of stitch	SSK	slip, slip, knit these 2 stitches together (*see above*)	YO	yarn over
K3tog	knit 3 stitches together						

Cables (Including without a Cable Needle)

Tutorials for 1 over 1 cables can be found at blog.knitpicks.com/tutorial-1-over-1-cables-without-a-cable-needle. Tutorials for standard cables can be found at blog.knitpicks.com/tutorial-introduction-to-cables.

Felted Join (to splice yarn)

One method for joining a new length of yarn to the end of one that is already being used. A tutorial can be found at tutorials.knitpicks.com/felted-join.

Mattress Stitch

A neat, invisible seaming method that uses the bars between the first and second stitches on the edges. A tutorial can be found at tutorials.knitpicks.com/mattress-stitch.

Provisional Cast On (crochet method)

Used to cast on stitches that are also a row of live stitches, so they can be put onto a needle and used later.
Directions: Using a crochet hook, make a slipknot, then hold knitting needle in left hand, hook in right. With yarn in back of needle, work a chain st by pulling yarn over needle and through chain st. Move yarn back to behind needle, and rep for the number of sts required. Chain a few more sts off the needle, then break yarn and pull end through last chain. (CO sts may be incorrectly mounted; if so, work into backs of these sts.) To unravel later (when sts need to be picked up), pull chain end out; chain should unravel, leaving live sts. A video tutorial can be found at tutorials.knitpicks.com/crocheted-provisional-cast-on.

Provisional Cast On (crochet chain method)

Same result as the crochet method above, but worked differently, so you may prefer one or the other.
Directions: With a crochet hook, use scrap yarn to make a slipknot and chain the number of sts to be cast on, plus a few extra sts. Insert tip of knitting needle into first bump of crochet chain. Wrap project yarn around needle as if to knit, and pull yarn through crochet chain, forming first st. Rep this process until you have cast on the correct number of sts. To unravel later (when sts need to be picked up), pull chain out, leaving live sts. A photo tutorial can be found at tutorials.knitpicks.com/crocheted-provisional-cast-on.

Judy's Magic Cast On

This method creates stitches coming out in opposite directions from a seamless center line, perfect for starting toe-up socks.
Directions: Make a slipknot and place loop around one of the two needles; anchor loop counts as first st. Hold needles tog, with needle that yarn is attached to on top. In other hand, hold yarn so tail goes over index finger and yarn attached to ball goes over thumb. Bring tip of bottom needle over strand of yarn on finger (top strand), around and under yarn and back up, making a loop around needle. Pull loop snug. Bring top needle (with slipknot) over yarn tail on thumb (bottom strand), around and under yarn and back up, making a loop around needle. Pull loop snug. Cont casting on sts until desired number is reached; top yarn strand always wraps around bottom needle, and bottom yarn strand always wraps around top needle. A tutorial can be found at tutorials.knitpicks.com/judys-magic-cast-on.

Stretchy Bind Off

Directions: K2, *insert LH needle into front of 2 sts on RH needle and knit them tog—1 st remains on RH needle. K1; rep from * until all sts have been bound off. A tutorial can be found at tutorials.knitpicks.com/go-your-own-way-socks-toe-up-part-7-binding-off.

Jeny's Surprisingly Stretchy Bind Off (for 1x1 Rib)

Directions: Reverse YO, K1, pass YO over; *YO, P1, pass YO and previous st over P1; reverse YO, K1, pass YO and previous st over K1; rep from * until 1 st is left, then break working yarn and pull it through final st to complete BO.

Kitchener Stitch (also called Grafting)

Seamlessly join two sets of live stitches together.
Directions: With an equal number of sts on two needles, break yarn leaving a tail approx four times as long as the row of sts, and thread through a blunt yarn needle. Hold needles parallel with WSs facing in and both needles pointing to the right. Perform Step 2 on the first front st, then Step 4 on the first back st, then continue from Step 1, always pulling yarn tightly so the grafted row tension matches the knitted fabric:
Step 1: Pull yarn needle K-wise through front st and drop st from knitting needle.
Step 2: Pull yarn needle P-wise through next front st, leaving st on knitting needle.
Step 3: Pull yarn needle P-wise through first back st and drop st from knitting needle.
Step 4: Pull yarn needle K-wise through next back st, leaving st on knitting needle.
Rep Steps 1-4 until all sts have been grafted together, finishing by working Step 1 through the last remaining front st, then Step 3 through the last remaining back st. Photo tutorials can be found at knitpicks.com/learning-center/learn-to-knit/kitchener.

Short Rows

There are several options for how to handle short rows, so you may see different suggestions/intructions in a pattern.
Wrap and Turn (W&T) (one option for Short Rows)
Work until the st to be wrapped. If knitting: Bring yarn to front, Sl next st P-wise, return yarn to back; turn work, and Sl wrapped st onto RH needle. Cont across row. If purling: Bring yarn to back of work, Sl next st P-wise, return yarn to front; turn work and Sl wrapped st onto RH needle. Cont across row.
Picking up Wraps: Work to wrapped st. If knitting: Insert RH needle under wrap, then through wrapped st K-wise; K st and wrap tog. If purling: Sl wrapped st P-wise onto RH needle, use LH needle to lift wrap and place it onto RH needle; Sl wrap and st back onto LH needle, and P tog.
A tutorial for W&T can be found at tutorials.knitpicks.com/short-rows-wrap-and-turn-or-wt.
German Short Rows (another option for Short Rows)
Work to turning point; turn. WYIF, Sl first st P-wise. Bring yarn over back of right needle, pulling firmly to create a "double stitch" on RH needle. If next st is a K st, leave yarn at back; if next st is a P st, bring yarn to front between needles. When it's time to work into double st, knit both strands tog.

THIS COLLECTION FEATURES

Billow™
Bulky Weight
100% Pima Cotton

Comfy™
Fingering & Worsted Weight
75% Pima Cotton, 25% Acrylic

Comfy™ Color Mist
Worsted Weight
75% Pima Cotton, 25% Acrylic

CotLin™
DK Weight
70% Tanguis Cotton, 30% Linen

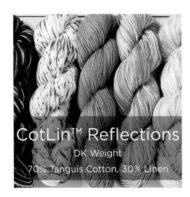

CotLin™ Reflections
DK Weight
70% Tanguis Cotton, 30% Linen

Lindy Chain™
Fingering Weight
70% Linen, 30% Pima Cotton

Shine™
Sport & Worsted Weight
60% Pima Cotton, 40% Modal®

Simply Cotton™
Sport Weight
100% Organic Cotton

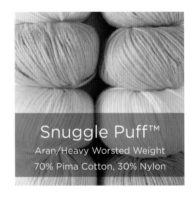

Snuggle Puff™
Aran/Heavy Worsted Weight
70% Pima Cotton, 30% Nylon

Knit Picks®

View these beautiful
yarns and more at
www.KnitPicks.com

Knit Picks yarn is both luxe and affordable—a seeming contradiction
trounced! But it's not just about the pretty colors; we also care
deeply about fiber quality and fair labor practices, leaving you with
a gorgeously reliable product you'll turn to time and time again.